The Value of You

THE GUIDE TO LIVING BOLDLY AND JOYFULLY THROUGH THE POWER OF CORE VALUES

Christopher D. Connors

Patricia William Publishing
New York

Contents

To Roman—

May you always believe in yourself

and have the courage to live the life of your dreams.

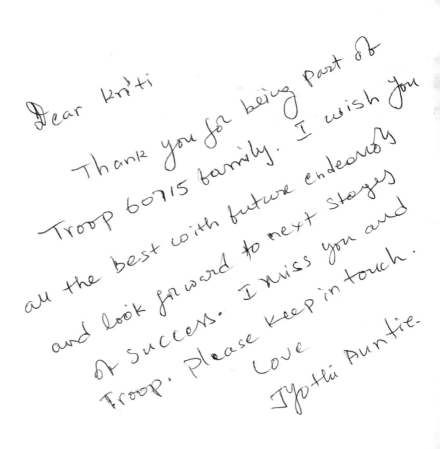

Dear Kriti

Thank you for being part of Troop 60715 family. I wish you all the best with future endeavors and look forward to next stages of success. I miss you and Troop. Please keep in touch.

Love

Jyothi Auntie-

CHAPTER 1

The Journey

"Your beliefs become your thoughts,
Your thoughts become your words,
Your words become your actions,
Your actions become your habits,
Your habits become your values,
Your values become your destiny."
— *Mahatma Gandhi*

Where are you going? Where have you been? **What are you doing about it?** Those were the questions that continued to pop into my mind. I wasn't happy with how things were going. So, I had a choice: sit there and do nothing, or rise up and begin the challenging—yet rewarding—work of reinventing myself and becoming the man I've always wanted to be. Seven years ago, I chose to begin the meaningful work of writing and living out my personal game plan. It has led to a bold new frontier of possibilities that never would have come my way had I stayed where I was.

I now pose these opening questions to you as you begin your work toward becoming the person you've always desired to be. Whether you're just out of college, a successful professional, struggling to find your way, single, or married with two children, understand this: When you seek to better yourself through a commitment to continuing education and personal development, you unlock the secret to a life of fulfillment and happiness. The surest way to achieve this is to begin with a rock-solid foundation—one built on core values.

Values are a set of guiding principles and ideals that provide a standard for the way we behave and make decisions. We choose to adhere to values because they positively influence our lives, leading us to the opportunities and relationships we desire.

All right, I've told you the "what." The goal of this book is to tell you the "*how-to*" for integrating values into your life. That is how you will maximize your potential. Isn't that why you're here? Actually, why are you here?! Was *Harry Potter and the Sorcerer's Stone* sold out on Amazon? Or did my mom send you? Maybe you're looking to take *your* big step toward becoming the woman or man you've always wanted to be. Whatever your reason, I'm grateful and encouraged you're along for the journey. I think you'll find that values give meaning and inspiration in helping us make sense of who we are and what we want to become.

The Case for Values

> *It is good to have an end to journey toward, but it is the journey that matters in the end." – Ursula Le Guin*

My thinking on values began after graduate school, in McLean, Virginia, at the headquarters of the management consulting firm where I worked.

On the first day of orientation, when everyone was still groggy-eyed and caffeine-deprived, the facilitator provided a history of the business, and then dove into the firm's core values. I was familiar with family values and why they mattered, but I had never paid much attention to a company, school or organization's values. I never considered the importance of values relative to running a business. Yet this company made it clear that values were essential for their success, and for each employee's advancement at the company. Not only would our superiors be judging our performance by these core values, so would our clients. In fact, promotions, pay increases and awards would be determined by how we represented the core values of the firm.

It all seemed a little too much like corporate hogwash to my—admittedly, too cynical—27-year-old self. Really? Promotions and pay increases tied to a few clichéd values like trust and teamwork? Ha! Right, sure. *Let's kiss up a bit and watch that VP promotion roll in!* So, I thought. But as I found along the way, values like respect and integrity were embedded in the thinking of my colleagues.

From that day forward, I started to think more about values. This thinking has stayed with me ever since. I wondered why values stand the test of time, and why people who live a values-based life are admired and honored by their peers and society. I learned that values-based living means practicing rigorous discipline and dedication to a core set of ideals and principles. Guiding values like perseverance, fire, and hope bring passion to our lives, leading us to achieve our goals. A values-based life shows belief—belief in others, belief in ourselves, and perhaps even belief in a power far greater than ourselves.

The truth is that many organizations don't have core values. Great ones do. Jim Collins, author of the bestselling book, *Built to Last*, wrote, "Companies that enjoy enduring success have a core purpose and core values that remain fixed while their strategies and practices endlessly adapt to a changing world." [1]

This same concept can be applied by people. Sadly, the truth is that most people don't live by core values. Many of us could easily rattle off a list of values like hard work, honesty, courage or integrity. Great start! But could we go further and think deeper about the driving forces in our lives? Could we share why we choose to integrate competitive greatness into our values structure? Or how living a disciplined life leads to greater peace of mind and less stress? As I've found in coaching executives, business leaders and students, the answer is "No."

This is especially true of millennials and young adults. Many are bright, bold, idealistic, and adventurous beyond measure! But many of us lack direction. We're full of ideas and bursting with excitement that often gets misplaced because we don't know the purpose for our lives. Values are the secret that give meaning and provide clarity to all these things.

Tired of Lukewarm

What values do you currently turn to for guidance? Do you find yourself referring to a particular set of values? Do you think of a talk from your parents, wisdom learned in the classroom, or a lesson you received in the "school of hard knocks"? You may be relying on values like humility and faith, without giving it much thought. Or perhaps there was a turning point in your life that caused you to think and find deeper meaning.

Values cut across age, class, race, ethnicity, and politics. Values like love, altruism and respect are honored by all people. They are a standard by which we measure ourselves. They determine what activities, jobs, and people we want to be a part of our life.

Without a firm, bedrock structure of values in place, my life would lack direction. I know this, because for too long, this was precisely the case. I was breezing through life, at times aimlessly, not knowing why I felt unfulfilled in my personal life and career. I kept making the same mistakes. I feared commitment and, as a result, I was indecisive. My relationships suffered, which further compounded a feeling of self-doubt. I needed foresight—a game plan to get me on track. I craved structure, yet my actions often had me flying by the seat of my pants.

What I lacked in maturity and answers, I made up for in intellectual curiosity and a desire to learn more about myself. I wanted to make sense of my subconscious thoughts, to possess bolder confidence and belief in myself, and to achieve peace of mind and results I could be proud of. I became a voracious reader. I started talking less and listening more. I began to find deeper meaning in my past. I came to peace with my regrets and mistakes, my insecurities, doubts, and fears. I realized I always had control over two very powerful things: my attitude and my effort. My attitude would shape my confidence and belief in myself, opening me up to new relationships and opportunities. My effort would be the driver to achieve my desires.

I used my professional training in management consulting and project management to write my definition of success and the "*Why*" for my life:

MY DEFINITION OF SUCCESS:

To live each moment to the maximum with a positive attitude, smile, and genuine enjoyment for life, while loving my family and the people around me, and pursuing the plan and dreams that God has placed in my heart.

MY WHY:

To help others and make a tangible difference in their lives through my writing, speaking, and coaching.

I realized that living these out meant applying values to all that I do. It was a gradual learning process, rather than a "Big-bang" approach. My "Why" and definition of success gave me clarity, structure, and firm direction—things I previously lacked. This led to establishing my personal core values. My values are derived from what I was taught by my parents, brothers, and extended family, as well as what I've learned on my journey through playing sports, coaching, schooling, and the workplace. They are also from numerous personal development, business, and creative books, as well as the teachings of Jesus Christ and lessons from the Bible.

The lessons and stories in this book are not the result of an "aha!" moment. They don't stem from one seminal experience like getting fired or learning of a diagnosis of a fatal disease. Rather, this book is the distillation of my years of experience living in the world while trying to find proven techniques and a foundational structure that gets results and provides peace of mind.

Values Are Forever

> " *Here are the values that I stand for. I stand for honesty, equality, kindness, compassion, treating people the way you want to be treated, and helping those in need. To me those are traditional values. That's what I stand for.*" – Ellen DeGeneres

A term that's familiar in investing parlance is "Buy and hold." As we saw with the dot-com bubble of the early 2000s and the recent *Great Recession*, that's not always the best advice. Life is filled with adversity and challenges. Financial decisions, as well as many life decisions, come at us quickly. We must be prepared to act swiftly, change course and make adjustments. Values position us for success and help us to make these moves.

Values are best suited to follow a mantra of "Embrace, adopt, and hold." Values are not temporary. Values are forever. Their constancy is their value. This permits us to recognize values as a standard to live by and aspire to. Values are the eternal spring we come to for life-giving water and renewal, no matter our personality, financial status, hair color, location, or religion.

There has been a lot of change in my life. Chances are, there has been in yours, as well. There's no doubt more change will come as you navigate the course of your dreams. As much as we try to delude ourselves at times, particularly when things are going great, time stops for no one. Our loved ones, friends, and heroes will all die. Our jobs will change. We may get laid off, or switch positions every couple years. Our moods will change. Places change. You might have moved this year. Maybe you left your parents' place for the first time.

You just found your brand-new apartment in Philly or San Francisco. Maybe in London or Sydney. Awesome!

As your journey continues, values become the compass that guides you and provides you direction. Values are to your personal development as the abdominal core is to your physical movement. The more you exercise and build up your core, the better equipped you are for movement and direction. In a similar way, your values become your core. They are the launching pad for how you grow and behave, both in public and when no one is watching.

Even as I write this book, I believe there are values I will add to my structure as I grow. This book is definitely not the sum total of values, nor does it include all of the values I put into practice and cherish. The values I discuss here are the ones I consider most essential for anyone looking to live a successful, fulfilling and purpose-driven life.

Hold on tight to the values you inherited—and continue to inherit—from family, school, friends, heroes, and role models. Pay close attention and listen. (Listening is, in fact, a value!) When you seek the truth, you must listen intently. Listen with your eyes and ears. Always seek to learn and grow in every experience that you have. That interview you didn't want to take could lead to a new opportunity worth its weight in gold. The lecture you didn't think you'd drop in on, after a long day of work, may provide you with the wisdom that serves as the impetus for a newfound dream.

Picking Ourselves Up

I'm no sage "values guru" with scrolls of rich text, living in a hut on a scenic mountaintop. Far from it! I've made mistakes and will continue to fall flat on my face at times. I'm a work in progress, just like all of us. As a result, I don't judge, knowing that I've failed and fallen short of the high standards that I set for myself. To do so is human. As Alfred says to Bruce Wayne in *Batman Begins*: "Why do we fall? So that we can learn to pick ourselves up."

I simply believe there is a code of values we all can live by that will add tremendous joy, love, and peace to our lives. We will fall short time and again, but we should never fail to get up. Rather, we should rise to our feet with confidence in our thoughts and inspiration in our hearts. We'll make improvements and keep growing that way.

The Breakdown

This book contains twenty values chapters which are broken down into five sections:

- Believe

- Heart

- Character

- Spirit

- Mindfulness

They can be read one at a time or straight through. The choice is yours, though I recommend using this as a values reference book.

You may find at different times that you need a boost in confidence, a shot of hope, or a simple reminder to have fun. You can begin right at that chapter to maximize your time and value. Think of this book as a kind of new-age encyclopedia. Remember when your friend up the street had one of those *World Book* encyclopedia libraries in their den? Now, all you need is your Kindle or this paperback, and you've got it made, my friend!

Each chapter is broken down into the following bite-sized sequence for easy readability:

- A quote about the value

- A definition of the value

- A story of someone, or an anecdote, that embodies the value

- The "core" of what the value is all about

- Obstacles to living the value

- The "value within the value," which dives deeper into the best way to practice this value, along with some stories to tell

- Results of living the value

- A Game Plan for you to put the value into practice

I will share stories from successful people throughout history, amazing stories from people who are lesser known, but no less significant, and lessons from my own life journey. I will provide you with step-by-step guidance for personal development in each value. Knowing about these values isn't enough. Living them is where you go for the win.

Onward to Victory

I turn back to the beginning questions of this chapter: Where are you going? Where have you been? *What are you doing about it?* As you think through these questions, I implore you to step up and take action; not out of duty or obligation, but out of a burning desire to find happiness and success. Go find your calling to become the person you are destined to be. Just know this—it's not only about the end goal. It's about the journey you take to get there. Because it's that journey that shapes, molds, and defines you in the end.

We become the sum of the parts of our personal experiences. I encourage you to take inventory and look back at all you've started, where you are now, and what's to come. Don't lose sight of the progress you've made. Keep pushing forward to the finish line on this marathon of life. It's not a sprint. Keep going! There's work to do.

I close with words from the greatest athlete I've ever seen, Michael Jordan. His story is told in two chapters of this book. Michael Jordan wasn't the greatest because he was the most talented. He wasn't perfect. He got knocked down repeatedly and chose to get up each time. He failed many times, so that he could succeed triumphantly. He once said, "I've failed over and over and over again in my life. And that is why I succeed."

You'll always succeed when you build your life on a strong foundation of core values. It is here that the journey truly begins to living the life of your dreams.

Notes

[1] Jim Collins and Jerry I. Porras, "Building Your Company's Vision," *Harvard Business Review,* September/October 1996 Issue, https://hbr.org/1996/09/building-your-companys-vision (accessed June 10, 2017).

I
Believe

CHAPTER 2

Faith

*"Faith is a grand cathedral, with divinely pictured windows -
standing without, you can see no glory, nor can imagine any,
but standing within every ray of light reveals a harmony of un-
speakable splendors."* [1]

— *Nathaniel Hawthorne*

<u>DEFINITION:</u>

*1a) Allegiance to a duty or person (b) 1. Fidelity to one's promises
(2): sincerity of intentions 2a (1): belief and trust in and loyalty to
God* [2]

The real-life story of Sylvester Stallone appears, at first glance, to be
as fictional as the screenplay he wrote for the movie *Rocky*. The now-
legendary movie catapulted him to fame and has defined his career.
Even forty years later, Stallone is the eternal Hollywood underdog
who epitomizes positive attitude, hard work, and faith in himself.

What a lot of people don't know about the man who is now a
multi-millionaire is that he had very few breaks. In fact, he was a
dead-broke actor in his mid-twenties. Stallone took on movie roles
more to survive than anything else. He was homeless for periods of

time and found himself sleeping in the Port Authority Bus Terminal in Midtown Manhattan. (As a native New Yorker, I assure you, that is not the most welcoming place to rest your head at night.)

Stallone would often roam into the New York Public Library on cold days just to keep warm. It was there that he began reading famous works of well-known literary titans like Edgar Allan Poe and Leo Tolstoy. Reading these books gave him hope. It served as inspiration for future writing, which would help him for his golden screenplay. But Stallone was still a few years away from reaching the big time—still poor, still desperate.

How desperate? Stallone hawked his wife's jewelry for money. Want more desperate? Out of despair, he sold his dog for $50. Imagine having to sell your dog—for $50! That's how dire his circumstances were. Despite having empty pockets, though, he never lost faith.

There's always a reason to believe.

Given his poverty, it's easy to think Stallone was looking for—perhaps even willing to settle on—any kind of break. A deal for something bigger? Well, that would be a no-brainer. After writing the screenplay for *Rocky*, he was able to find Hollywood studios interested in his script. This alone was a break some live their whole life hoping to find. However, Stallone didn't just want to be the writer. He believed that he should *play* Rocky Balboa! Oh, the arrogance!

The *chutzpah*!

Ah, the confidence. The resolve. The belief. The impenetrable faith.

Stallone refused to compromise, even to the tune of $300,000, saying No to A-list Hollywood actors Robert Redford and Burt Reynolds for the lead role of Rocky Balboa. Stallone believed the role was his. Keep in mind, the man was destitute and had just sold his dog. The $300,000 he'd been offered would be the modern-day equivalent of approximately $1.2 million[3] — an offer most anyone would immediately jump at. But not Stallone.

It would take perseverance and unrelenting willpower to continue pushing himself and his idea in front of Hollywood producers. Stallone had a vision, which he backed with faith—the belief that he would be the one to star in Rocky. So, there was no deal to be had. Eventually, to star in his own movie, he sold his script for far less money—$25,000 to be exact. Once Stallone got the money for the film, he got his dog back, who went on to appear in the movie. Stallone never stopped believing. It paid off.

"On a slim $1,075,000 production budget, 'Rocky' went on to earn more than $117 million in the U.S. alone. The six-part 'Rocky' franchise has since brought in more than a billion dollars worldwide." [4]

"[Rocky] won the Academy Award for best picture in 1976. At the awards ceremony [Stallone] read out all the rejection slips from those who said the film would be sappy, predictable and a film that no one would want to watch." [5]

In many ways, Stallone was already a success. He grinded, staying up late hours and never quitting. He believed he would find success on his terms. His faith was justified, leading to a remarkable new reality. We can only imagine how he felt in those moments, where it would have been so easy to give up his hope of acting, to pitch his screenplay and find a new fortune. The man was pawning his wife's jewelry for goodness' sake! Yet somehow, some way, the timing wasn't yet right. He wanted more, and he wouldn't be denied.

What are you facing in your life at this moment that is causing you fear, uncertainty, or doubt? None of those things are any match for the power of faith. Life reminds us at every moment of adversity, every time of victory—and everything in between—that we must believe in ourselves and our future. Faith is what makes everything possible. Even when we're an underdog, we can fight our way to the top.

The Core of Faith

You might be thinking, why is faith the first value chapter in this book? Is there a reason for that? Did Chris just randomly shuffle the chapters like an iPod? Did he ask his toddler son to pick the winner out of a hat? Actually, this book begins with faith, because faith is the foundation of my values structure. Faith is a major reason why I chose to write this book.

Everything in my life, the person I am and desire to be, is because of faith. I believe you'll find the same applies to you. Allow me to explain.

We are what we think. The world we create begins in our mind. Our thoughts influence and color our entire existence. If you believe you can become an actor, to borrow the words of President Theodore Roosevelt, "you're halfway there." While we are social creatures who are influenced by the people and things around us, we are always in control of our thoughts. Our attitude and effort are linked to the way we think. The way we think is imbued by the faith that we have in ourselves.

Everything begins with a thought, which is then backed by desire and empowered by faith. Take a few minutes to think about the thoughts that occupy your mind. What do you truly want most in life? What things provide the most meaning and value to you?

You may want to be a pediatrician someday. An amazing ambition. The idea for this first enters your mind as a thought. The more you think about it, if it resonates with you, if it's part of your destiny, then you begin to derive a pure, natural desire for that goal. Those thoughts become dominating thoughts which continue to enter your mind in a positive, exciting way.

From that point, whether you realize it or not, you hit a key decision point. You can back that thought and desire with faith, or you can let it die. If you choose the path of faith, you'll need to believe in yourself! Your faith will fuel your confidence, which gives you the assurance that you are following the right path and that you can be a pediatrician. Without faith, you will not achieve your dream.

My faith is comprised of three things: belief in God, belief in others, and belief in myself. I learned during my twenties, after lots of trial and error, that if I ever wanted to live life on my terms and be truly free, I needed to believe in myself and what I could achieve. The more I've studied faith and made sense of my own, I've come to realize that faith is essential for living a life of value, happiness, and peace of mind. If we don't believe in something, how can we ever take steps forward with confidence and courage?

A lack of faith leads to fear. When we're afraid, we're hesitant to give things a shot. Fear blocks us. It limits our confidence. This may hinder our chance to land that dream social media job at Facebook, or prevent us from asking out our crush on a date. To some degree, we all have faith. Faith enables us to do things like drive a car on a busy highway. When we speak up for ourselves or an idea, we're showing faith. All our actions are preceded by faith!

Obstacles to Living with Faith

" *Remember: we all get what we tolerate. So stop tolerating excuses within yourself, limiting beliefs of the past, or half-assed or fearful states."* [6] *—Tony Robbins*

- Limiting beliefs

- Negative mindset

- Feeling like you're stuck

- Feeling like you have nothing to look forward to

- Difficult circumstances (misfortune in your life, uncertainty)

Where are you currently in your "faith life"? Ah, see, I threw a curve ball in there. For many people, faith and religion are inextricably linked, synonymous with one another as much as peanut butter is with jelly. Faith is often perceived in a religious context as the belief in a Higher Power, the dogma or adherence to a particular set of beliefs. As a result, it's often undervalued.

This chapter is not about religion. It's about the beliefs that shape your mind and, in turn, shape your life. Look back to the beginning of this chapter. See how the lovely folks at *Merriam-Webster* define faith. Notice, it isn't until the second definition of faith that we see any mention of God or the belief in doctrines of religion. In the first definition, the focus is on "fidelity to one's promises." In the second definition, I love the two words, "sincerity" and "trust." This is when we're on our game, integrating faith into our life. It is here that we believe, and do so with confidence.

A Story to Tell

" *Whether you think you can, or you think you can't—you're right."—Henry Ford*

I didn't believe I was ready. I didn't believe I could. So, I nearly missed out on the love of my life. That's the short version of how I lost my then-girlfriend, only to find her again. Two years before tying the knot, I broke up with my now-wife for what I thought was the final time. I simply didn't believe in myself enough. I was immature, selfish, and aimless in my direction. For the ensuing year, which at times felt like an eternity, I dove deep into my faith. I cut out a lot of "time wasters" like surfing the Internet, partying too often, and frankly, flying by the seat of my pants through life.

I began planning things out. I started asking a lot of questions and I did a lot of soul-searching. I got focused on what mattered most. My biggest turnaround was simply believing I was ready to be a husband, that I was ready to wholeheartedly embrace life's journey with her. It was faith first! It was the belief that we belonged together and that I had what it took to be her man.

So, I decided to go all-in and tried re-connecting with her. It wasn't easy, but gradually I won back her trust by demonstrating faith in her, as well as fidelity to myself. I stopped hindering my mind with limiting beliefs. The rest, as they say, is history. She gave me one final shot and we reunited in marriage. In the end, we both believed in one another. That power of faith was enough for us to each give love one more chance.

3 Questions on Faith to Ask Yourself:

1. What matters most to you—is it a person, your job or the pursuit of a dream? Whatever that something is, you must believe in it with all your mind, body and soul.

2. Do you dedicate time each day to prayer or meditation? Tap into your spiritual side!

3. What limiting belief is holding you back from being the person you want to be?

I've had plenty of conversations with friends and colleagues who—at some point—simply could not see a way forward. They were so focused on doubting themselves in the present. Their biggest enemy was the way they perceived themselves, or how their business associates and friends saw them. It took a step outside of their arena to realize how valued they were and to recognize how much they had accomplished. Then, they could better value themselves.

Limiting beliefs often arise when we are too tough on ourselves (like heaping on self-criticism when we don't get the promotion we've been eyeing for a year). Limiting your beliefs disrespects your past, and all you've accomplished. It undermines your present. It damages your future prospects, which are born from the confidence, daring, and faith of now.

Despite how much I write about faith as the foundation of our values structure, I'd be an impostor if I told you there aren't still times of doubt or negativity that creep into my life. All of us have these! It's the believers among us who reduce these times to mere passing moments—mile-markers on the highway that soon fade into our rear-view, as they give way to the vast new horizons on our landscape. Our future then unfolds with bold, empowering feelings of self-belief, self-motivation, and enthusiasm. From that vantage point, there's no limit to what you can do.

Value within the Value

" *RICHES begin in the form of THOUGHT! The amount is limited only by the person in whose mind the THOUGHT is put into motion. FAITH removes limitations! Remember this when you are ready to bargain with Life for whatever it is that you ask as your price."* [7] *— Napoleon Hill*

Most people interpret Napoleon Hill's use of the word "riches" as financial wealth. What he was really writing about was a series of qualities that form a composite set of "riches." Here are his twelve things:

The 12 Things Which Constitute Real Riches

1. A positive mental attitude

2. Sound physical health

3. Harmony in human relations

4. Freedom from fear

5. The hope of future achievement

6. The capacity for applied faith

7. Willingness to share one's blessings with others

8. To be engaged in the labor of love

9. An open mind on all subjects toward all people

10. Complete self-discipline

11. Wisdom with which to understand people

12. Financial security

Notice number one: a positive attitude. The capacity for applied faith comes in sixth, but look closer at all twelve things on this list. Only the last item, which is ranked last for a reason, is not a direct product of having faith. Faith is only possible when we have a positive attitude—not when we're negative! Faith opens our minds to opportunities and imagination. Opportunities lead to the probability that we will find what we're searching for and desiring. Faith leads to the belief that the pieces that are not already assembled in our lives will come together in due time.

Patience, a virtue that requires faith, dares us to live disciplined lives. Patience encourages us to believe that "our time" will come around. This is directly correlated to an outward expectation of future happiness. What's so hard about this trial of faith is the not-knowing. The late Tom Petty, if I may be so bold, was wrong. The waiting isn't the hardest part. It's the *not-knowing* that's the hardest part. Our generation has lost its faith as we've grown. We believe that things should always happen, right away. When they don't, many of us lose hope. As a result, we get discouraged.

How many people have you seen give up on dreams at precisely the moment when they should have "doubled down" on faith and given it their all?

That's a horrible, defeating, and destructive way to live! While I'm a huge proponent of living life on your terms, I draw a distinction between getting life to bow to your advantage and believing that time will always work in your favor. When we develop a values-based approach, predicated on time-tested qualities, we live life more and more on our terms. We believe in ourselves, and in others, and we keep moving forward in pursuit of the life we know is ours.

" *Faith is to believe what you do not see; the reward of this faith is to see what you believe."—St. Augustine*

We need to have faith and patience that our journey will find its successful end, as long as we've done all that we can to ensure victory. Yes, the timing is largely out of our control, but it's up to us to capitalize and focus on the things that are in our control. Faith enables the feeling that our future is in good hands.

One of the most powerful quotes of our lifetime was spoken by a true innovator and genius, Steve Jobs. He said,

> *You can't connect the dots looking forward; you can only connect them looking backwards. So you have to trust that the dots will somehow connect in your future. You have to trust in something—your gut, destiny, life, karma, whatever. This approach has never let me down, and it has made all the difference in my life.* [8]

Things will work out when they are supposed to. Understand that instant gratification is best left to the world of fantasy. Keep the faith! The secret is not to worry or despair that your reality hasn't aligned perfectly with your dreams. Remain calm. Connections and fortuitous alliances will happen, not when we think they should but, often when we least expect it. Focus on the things that require your attention and go out there and get what's yours!

Results of Faith

Faith is a knowledge within the heart, beyond the reach of proof.—Khalil Gibran

Without faith in ourselves, we wouldn't have the courage to love. I am living proof of this truth! We cannot give of ourselves to someone else—the precious sacrifice called love—without first imagining that it is possible. Then, we can believe it into being. Our thoughts give rise to our function. To commit to loving, we must first believe in what we're doing. This implies that we believe in ourselves and in the individual who will receive our love.

Start by speaking your faith over your life. Start by telling those you trust that you believe in them. Declare your faith in writing, in words, and show your faith through your actions. Visualize this connection before committing to the actions. The visualization of seeing your faith will help you. Faith results in an outlook that seeks to find a way, rather than making excuses or avoiding the truth. We have to believe that the things we desire—the things which are not yet seen—are not just possible, but that they will be ours.

There's always a reason to believe—in ourselves, in those we love and admire, and in causes that light the fire inside us and make us feel alive. I bet there's something you've been putting off for "the right time." What if I told you the right time is now! Believe that this year, this moment, is going to be one where you live in abundance. Then, take action to make it so.

Game Plan

1. Start thinking of faith in the context of faith in yourself, others, God, or perhaps fate or destiny. Place an emphasis on critical thinking, questioning why you believe what you do. Challenge your assumptions, ask questions and continue to refine your faith. Seek the truth!

2. Believe in yourself to follow the path that leads to achieving your goals. Be accepting that you won't understand or know in advance each step of the process. This is what faith is all about! You won't have all the answers. You won't control all the outcomes. Believe things will work out. Never doubt yourself, and of course never give up.

3.   You need to have blind faith about the things and people you believe in most. The "people" part should include you! Have the faith and courage to put all your chips in the center of the table. Do so only after you've first given things deep thought. Have your thoughts (which will soon become decisions) validated by someone very close to you, who you can trust. Then, give all you've got. I think you'll find, the issue is never the "doing." It's overcoming the fear. Faith smashes fear!

Notes

[1] Nathaniel Hawthorne, *The Marble Faun* (or *The Romance of Monte Benii*) (Boston: Ticknor and Fields, 1860).

[2] "Faith," *Merriam-Webster*, https://www.merriam-webster.com/dictionary/faith (accessed May 14, 2017).

[3] US Inflation Calculator, http://www.usinflationcalculator.com/.

[4] Aly Weisman, "Dirt-Poor Sylvester Stallone Turned Down $300,000 in 1976 To Ensure He Could Play 'Rocky,'" *Business Insider*, April 2, 2014, http://www.businessinsider.com/sylvester-stallone-made-rocky-against-all-odds-2014-4 (accessed May 14, 2017).

[5] 5"The Sylvester Stallone Story," *Sprint Ninja*, http://www.endlesshumanpotential.com/sylvester-stallone-story.html (accessed May 14, 2017).

[6] Tony Robbins, *MONEY: Master the Game: 7 Simple Steps to Financial Freedom* (NY: Simon & Schuster, 2014), 202.

[7] Napoleon Hill, *Think and Grow Rich* (Robbinsdale, MN: Fawcett Publications, 1937).

[8] Steve Jobs, Stanford University Commencement address, 2005, http://news.stanford.edu/2005/06/14/jobs-061505/ (accessed May 14, 2017).

CHAPTER 3

Hope

"Hope is being able to see that there is light despite all of the darkness."

— Desmond Tutu

<u>**DEFINITION:**</u>

To cherish a desire with anticipation: to want something to happen or be true

To desire with expectation of obtainment or fulfillment; to expect with confidence: trust [1]

Happiness and achievement are in direct proportion to the hope that lives in our hearts and minds. There is no story of personal success that better exemplifies this than the true story of a woman who spends her days writing about a fictional universe replete with a wizard named Dumbledore and a game called Quidditch. Her name is J. K. Rowling, and her emergence as one of the bestselling authors in history is nothing short of incredible.

If all you know of her is the name you see at the bottom of each *Harry Potter* book cover, I invite you to learn more. She channeled and cultivated hope, which lifted her spirit and carried her from the precipice of despair to stunning new heights.

J. K. Rowling didn't have a top-notch Oxford education. She was a good student, but she lacked a clear path for her life upon graduation from university. She bounced around from job-to-job for a few years. At age twenty-five, in the summer of 1990, Rowling was hunting for an apartment in Manchester, England, with her then-boyfriend. She was still living in London at the time and working as a bilingual secretary.

After a weekend of searching to find a place to live, she traveled back to London. During a delayed train trip, a dynamic, life-changing idea came to her. Suddenly like magic, the idea for Harry Potter "came fully formed into her mind."

"All of a sudden the idea for Harry just appeared in my mind's eye. I can't tell you why or what triggered it. But I saw the idea of Harry and the wizard school very plainly. I suddenly had this basic idea of a boy who didn't know who he was, who didn't know he was a wizard until he got his invitation to wizard school. I have never been so excited by an idea."
[2] *—J. K. Rowling*

Not long after the incredible idea for Harry Potter appeared in her mind, Rowling's mother died. Her death would have an enormous impact on the formation of Rowling's goals. Rowling knew she needed to press on with her idea, give it life, and let it transform her world. She ended her relationship, and later moved to Porto, Portugal, to teach English.

It was there she would meet her future husband and have a child, though her marriage would last only thirteen months. Rowling lived with tremendous stress, often questioning herself. She endured terrible physical and emotional abuse. Her move to southern Europe ended in misery.

" *Rock bottom became the solid foundation on which I rebuilt my life." – J. K. Rowling*

She relocated to Edinburgh, Scotland, hoping to begin anew and raise her young daughter. By this time, she was a single mother, living off state benefits in the United Kingdom. She pinched pennies, buying only cheap food and clothes for herself and her daughter. She viewed herself as a failure.[3] Both personally and professionally, it was a bitter fall for a woman who had high expectations of herself.

How dire did her situation get? She was clinically diagnosed with depression and even thought about taking the gravest action possible—committing suicide. Yet incredibly, her drastic circumstances led her to write more and more. She used this period of depression to muster up the courage to keep going. Everything in her life seemed dark and dismal, yet there was still hope.

During this time, Rowling continued to believe in her idea and her ability to turn it into something special. Over the next few years, she penned the first *Harry Potter* novel. Success did not come right away. First, Rowling's manuscript was rejected by several literary agents. It was finally accepted by Christopher Little Literary Agents. The agency then sent out her manuscript to twelve different publishers.

All of them rejected the manuscript.

Finally, Bloomsbury accepted it. After eighteen months, and tons of rejection, Rowling's persistence and resolve won the day. *Harry Potter and the Philosopher's Stone* (known in the U.S. as *Harry Potter and the Sorcerer's Stone*) was published in June 1997. Since the book's release, Rowling has become one of the richest and most successful women in the world.

In her late twenties J. K. Rowling ended up destitute. She was on welfare benefits, heartbroken, divorced, beaten down and with her life falling apart. So, she decided to do what she does best to lift herself out of misfortune and failure. She began writing. She never lost hope. It has made all the difference in her remarkable journey.

The Core of Hope

> *Hope's highest manifestation is the perseverance of the soul who has seen a better day, who has a tangible sense of what satisfied feels like, who knows that the reality of their today dims into a pale insignificance when compared to the radiant, the incandescent promise of tomorrow."—Wayne Abel, The New Hope Times*

Hope is born from faith. Faith starts this amazing process in our mind, which takes our ideas, gives them life, then propels us into hoping for what we believe in. When we have hope, we begin to develop a passion that leads to love—love for another, a cause, pursuit, or goal that we desire. Hope is a prodigious power that forges forward, elevating our mental, emotional, physical, and spiritual state. Hope elevates us in lean times and sustains us in times of joy. This is heavy stuff. Is your heart beating fast? So is mine.

Let's break down the wanting and thinking parts of hope: To want something is to desire it—to have a visualized, favorable view of something. This desire continues to increase your affinity for that object in the hope that you may someday have it. To think on something is to first conjure up an image of it in your mind. Next, you use the power of your mind to believe something is true or that something will become true. To desire something, you first have to use your imagination.

Think about your big dream—let me know how the view looks from your Houston skyscraper once you make partner at a prestigious law firm. Send me a copy of your first book once you hit the NYT Bestseller List. What is it for you? How often do you imagine this?

Hope is fueled by our creative imagination, which then manifests itself in the indomitable power of our will. It is through this willpower (which we all have) and optimism that we blend perseverance and persistence. Hope and perseverance go hand in hand! Our hope must persevere, otherwise it cannot bring our desire to fruition. Hope is not ephemeral, rather, it is everlasting. It carries us throughout our life. It begins on the playgrounds and soccer fields, and in the classroom.

A study from University of Kansas researchers shows that hope is also linked to academic success in college. According to Dr. Charles Snyder and his colleagues:

Researchers looked at the impact of hope on college academic achievement over the course of 6 years. Hope was related to a higher

GPA 6 years later, even after taking into account the original GPA and ACT entrance examination scores of the participants. High hope students (relative to low hope students) were also more likely to have graduated and were less likely to be dismissed from school due to bad grades.[4]

Hope is the shining light that allows us to see our goals. Hope is future-seeking, it requires vision and foresight. Hope is about wanting things so badly, with burning desire and passion, that you will your mind to believe you will get what you want. Whether that's a new car, a better life for your children, or the hope of having a first child, hope is sincere, pure, and filled with anticipation.

Anxiety, worry, and fear can rob us of joy in the moment, but hope always perseveres in the long run. Our future thoughts should be sprinkled with hope—a belief the best is yet to come. During moments of doubt in your life, I encourage you to hold out hope that things will improve. Hope is an enduring flame that lights the way for us, through a power that is our own—that no one can or ever will take away.

Obstacles to Living with Hope

- Lack of vision

- Anxiety and doubt

- Despair

- Bad break or adversity

- Previous failures

The obstacles to hope focus around an inability to imagine a future destiny in line with our dreams. As you've seen, we will all encounter adversity. It gets harder to hope when we've failed—particularly when we've failed many times. This is precisely when anxiety can set in, which at its worst leads to despair. While suffering is a part of life, none of us should wallow in doubt, fear, and worry for too long.

Drugs, alcohol, depressants, hanging around with negative people, these are all obstacles to achieving what you hope to have in life. These things activate or prolong periods of hurt and pain. When you're stuck in neutral or surrounded by negative things, you tend to stop thinking big ideas. You're less inspired. Inspiration is vital to imagination! It helps us envision the things we want.

I ask you to think in the context of your life—what are the obstacles holding you back from having hope today? What are you doing about it?

We've all experienced painful breakups that turn our worlds upside down. A loss of a job or worst yet—a family member—sends shockwaves through our emotional world. It is hope that gets us back on our feet.

Living a values-based life continues the habit of making good deposits into our life's piggy bank. Think of this from a subtraction and addition perspective. The more you have hope, the more those accounts will continue to increase. You'll eliminate negative behaviors and thinking. The net effect will serve as compound interest that continues to grow in the form of self-satisfaction and peace of mind. You'll be able to weather the bad times that will inevitably come, and you'll come out stronger on the other end.

Value within the Value

Start with your thoughts. Think big, deep thoughts and write down your goals in small, incremental measures. Before long, you'll have a plan you can be proud of. Your goals and dreams can begin to take shape and materialize as you steel your resolve to accomplish them. Don't give in to self-criticism or the criticism of others. And, equally important, avoid jealous or envious thinking at all costs! Hope is the antithesis of negative thinking.

Speaking our dreams and goals over our lives strikes a verbal contract of accountability. Many people run away from their dreams and lose hope because they're afraid of what others might think of them. For far too long, I was a living example of this. I was afraid to be vulnerable in my writing. I was afraid to tell others what I really wanted to achieve in life. It took overcoming insecurity and fear to even speak about my personal struggles with my wife! But once I did, it blasted open the door to interior freedom, courage, and self-confidence. It was empowering, and it fueled the hope I needed to keep doing the same thing in the future.

Once I started telling people the desires of my heart, I started moving in the right direction. I urge you to take your thoughts and convert them into words with someone—or several people—whom you trust. Hope is the change agent that emotionalizes your thoughts and words and furthers your desire for fulfillment, happiness, and success.

A Story to Tell

" *Any idea, plan, or purpose may be placed in the mind through repetition of thought."—Napoleon Hill*

This is a story I know well. It's the story of my dear friend, my brother and mentor, Kevin. These days my brother is seen on national television five nights each week on ESPN. He's a broadcast journalist and celebrity in his own right. Everything he has can be attributed to his natural talents, perseverance, faith and hope. Kevin worked hard

until he reached the pinnacle of his profession. He made it to the top because he envisioned himself getting there. He dreamed big dreams. He had the mindset of a winner. But keep in mind, Kevin's success did not come overnight.

Kevin Connors and Mike Wilbon. Photo Courtesy: Kevin Connors

Kevin knew when he was in 8th grade what he wanted to do professionally. He started announcing sports scores over the intercom at our middle school. He did the same in high school. Kevin used his basketball-playing ability to earn an athletic scholarship at the college level, where he attended a school with one of the top Radio & TV programs in the United States. After graduation, he launched what has become a 20-year career in sports broadcasting. He busted his tail for nine long years at a regional television station, hoping to make the big time. There were moments of doubt and frustration. Kevin dreamed of being on national television. But it seemed so far away.

He concentrated on getting better each day. He surrounded himself with inspiring thoughts, stories, and images of fellow broadcasters who made the big time, as well powerful stories of athletes. He kept going. Kept believing. Kept hoping. Finally, his big break came in 2006 when he accepted a job with WCBS-Radio in New York. Less than one year later, he was working on television for WCBS-TV. And in 2008, he reached the big time: eleven years after graduating college, hoping his dream would come true, Kevin received an offer to work at the worldwide leader of sports, ESPN.

Chances are, you will not find success or personal fulfillment in your first job. That's OK! Few people are blessed with both the talent and foresight to know precisely what they want to do with their lives right after college. Even fewer people have this ability at a young age. My brother, Kevin, is one of those lads who did know. It's worked out for him. Things work out for all of us when we give light to the burning flame of hope. As Tim Robbins' character, Andy Dufresne, says in *The Shawshank Redemption*, "Hope is a good thing, maybe the best of things, and no good thing ever dies."

Results of Hope

You have a unique story to share with the world. Where are you on your journey? Are you going through the doldrums of doubt and fear? Do you see the proverbial light at the end of the tunnel—the end-vision of your goal? Perhaps your path is as open as the Pacific Coast Highway at sunrise in Laguna Beach. Maybe it's a Midtown Manhattan traffic jam. It's all a state of mind. You need inspiration and hope to create the beautiful landscapes of limitless possibility in your mind, which serve as the foundation for life's magical journeys. You are the creator of your world. When you are safe in the knowledge that you control your worldly destiny, nothing will ever stop you.

> *Great are they who see that spiritual is stronger than any material force—that thoughts rule the world."—Ralph Waldo Emerson*

I've got a long way to go. Chances are, so do you. The way to cultivate and build momentum is through inspiration—the power of hope. It becomes truer for me by the day that we control our own destiny through the power of our thoughts. We emotionalize our ideas with the power of love, faith, and hope. We take these thoughts and envision ourselves doing what we desire. Then, we make a plan and take the action that we've dreamed of. It really is that simple.

There is no shame in any idea, as long as you believe it will add value to your life and the lives of others. Don't concern yourself with the brilliance of your idea. Your race, your cause, is the one that speaks to the desires and dreams of your heart. That's what makes you unique and special. Be inspired and start doing simple things.

Saint Francis of Assisi once said, "Start by doing what's necessary; then do what's possible; and suddenly you are doing the impossible."

Our imagination empowers us, leading us to hope. We have this power inside of us every day. We share the power to hope for better things for ourselves and the world, here in the present and in the future.

I'll close with the words of Ms. Rowling:

Imagination is not only the uniquely human capacity to envision that which is not, and therefore the fount of all invention and innovation. In its arguably most transformative and revelatory capacity, it is the power that enables us to empathize with humans whose experiences we have never shared. Unlike any other creature on this planet, humans can learn and understand, without having experienced. They can think themselves into other people's places. We do not need magic to change the world, we carry all the power we need inside ourselves already: we have the power to imagine better.[5]

Game Plan

1. What are your current roadblocks to happiness? Identify them and come up with a solution for exactly how you plan to overcome them. Once you start putting the wheels in motion to overcome negativity and insert positivity, you've built up hope. From there, you need to sustain that hope by continuing forward with living out your solution.

2. Develop a daily inspirational routine. Make your routine an everyday thing. Here's how:

    a. Dedicate 10 minutes of contemplation time, alone in solitude, at the beginning of each day. Close your eyes. Begin to focus your thoughts on positive, stimulating things such as: love for your girlfriend/boyfriend, wife or husband; music; friendship and winning in your personal and professional life. Envision yourself attaining success or fame. There's tremendous power that comes through visualization. To believe something will happen, you have to envision it happening. Envision yourself standing in the "winner's circle" and someday, you'll be there.

    b. Write down the positive thoughts that come to mind. Keep referring back to them throughout your day by dedicating five-minute "time-outs" to reflect on all the positive things in your life. Think of them during a quick water break, during moments of difficulty or times of joy. Look at them again before you go to bed at night and reset your mind. Then, rest and get ready for the new day with excitement, anticipation, and a clear mind for fresh, new thoughts.

Notes

[1] "Hope," *Merriam-Webster*, https://www.merriam-webster.com/dictionary/hope (accessed May 24, 2017).

[2] Marc Shapiro, *J.K. Rowling: The Wizard Behind Harry Potter (via School Library Journal* conversation); (St. Martin's Griffin: New York, NY, 2001)

[3] "J.K. Rowling Biography: Success Story of the 'Harry Potter' Author," *Astrum People*, https://astrumpeople.com/jk-rowling/ (accessed May 24, 2017).

[4] Scott Barry Kaufman, Ph.D., "The Will and Ways of Hope," *Psychology Today*, December 26, 2011, https://www.psychologytoday.com/blog/beautiful-minds/201112/the-will-and-ways-hope (accessed May 24, 2017).

[5] Charlotte Whistlecroft, "Harry Potter author JK Rowling's Christmas message of hope is what the world really needs right now," *Digital Spy*, December 24, 2016, http://www.digitalspy.com/showbiz/harry-potter/news/a817739/harry-potter-author-jk-rowling-twitter-christmas-message/ (accessed May 24, 2017).

CHAPTER 4

Confidence

*"I was raised with confidence. I've never had a voice telling
me, 'You can't do this.' I've always believed I can do it."*

— *Amy Schumer*

DEFINITION:

*A feeling or consciousness of one's powers or of reliance on one's
circumstances; faith or belief that one will act in a right, proper, or
effective way.*[1]

Not long after returning home from graduating college, I got a call
from an old friend. "Come in to the city to see me! I have to show
you something!" The excitement in her voice pulsated through the
receiver. This must be good, I thought. I took the Long Island Rail
Road into New York and looked forward to my surprise. My friend
had studied acting in college and graduated with a degree in theater.
I figured she was ecstatic to show me some of the new material she
was working on. She had started to learn the tricks of the trade and
was thrilled to share her passion with me.

The *something* happened to be a performance. The visual proof
was on VHS tape (these weren't the days of Blu-Ray). We snuck into

one of those old-school New York electronics stores, a true relic from the past, and she slipped the tape into the VCR and pressed play. The video came on. I watched my friend performing, entertaining and doing what she loved. I turned to her and could see the gleam in her eye. I got that special feeling you get when you see someone truly immersed in a moment, enthralled with that thing they love most in the world. Enthusiasm. Pride. Confidence. She had it all then, and she certainly does now.

Amy Schumer is a good friend of mine. We've known each other since the third grade. We ran cross country together, played basketball, went to movies and school fairs, and hung out frequently in our high school years. Today she is one of the biggest stars in film and TV. It's been spectacular to watch someone I've known most of my life ascend to the mountaintop of stardom, achieving success beyond anyone's wildest dreams.

Amy is one of the most confident people I know. She didn't just stumble upon her place as one of the top entertainers in the world. It certainly wasn't luck that enabled her to write the script for the movie *Trainwreck*, in which she starred in the lead role. She grinded it out for years acting, honing her craft, and performing in comedy clubs across the United States. The diligence, dedication, and effort she put in has transformed her into a confident, self-assured woman whose platform has enabled her to lend an empowering voice to millions of women.

I watched with pride as she blossomed and came into her own on the NBC show, *Last Comic Standing*. This was her coming out party—an opportunity to show the world how talented she was. She nailed it. But that was in 2007. It would take several more years before she earned her own show on Comedy Central and became a household name. Before you get your own show, the big networks usually want to see a larger body of work. They don't hand shows out to just anybody! So, Amy kept plugging away. With each new accomplishment, she gained more confidence and greater validation in what she was doing.

A few years later, after enjoying more success and opportunities, she crushed it once again with her performance during the Comedy Central roast of Charlie Sheen. Amy knew it was her time to shine—and she owned it. This is the result of the time-tested formula of preparation meets opportunity.

These days, I can't seem to go to the pharmacy or grocery store without seeing her on the cover of a major magazine. Just remember—these kinds of rewards are the fruit of hard work and persistence. They take time. In Amy's case, it also took a support structure of family and friends—encouraging voices—that made her feel proud about the way she lives her life. As she's often told me, she thinks about self-confidence in the context of living each day with greater purpose and ambition. The impact she wants to leave on the world is one of speaking up for causes she believes in, like women's rights, and delivering her comedy in a way that is inspiring and, of course, funny.

As you plot your course in life, I encourage you to focus on growing your sense of self-worth and confidence. You can have all the talent in the world, but first, you must believe in your ability to succeed. You cannot let doubt creep into your mind and throw you off. Amy would be the first to tell you, the value of confidence has served as the foundation of her success.

From the days of telling jokes in grade school, to making 20,000 people laugh at Madison Square Garden, she's always had it.

The Core of Confidence

Confidence is a state of mind that can be cultivated through faith, self-motivating thought, repetition of actions, and reinforced by surrounding ourselves with positive, encouraging support. Confidence can be built and generated from within. It is derived from continuous learning and trial and error. Whereas leadership is the composite of skills acquired through experience, confidence is a state of mind, also shaped by our experiences.

In his excellent book, *Finding Your Zone* [2], Dr. Michael Lardon, M.D., focuses on the criteria and characteristics that drive peak performance. He uses examples of how we can channel our emotions to perform better, and details how desire can be transformed into empowering our will.

He also highlights psychologist Albert Bandura's four-step process [3] for developing confidence. The steps are:

1. Mastery Experiences

2. Vicarious Learning

3. Modeling Behavior

4. Social Persuasion

Mastery experiences consist of achieving successes—victories—then building upon those through perseverance and belief in self. The more you win, the more you believe you will continue to win, and your confidence levels increase. Vicarious learning involves learning from observing others, particularly your peers. When you participate in an activity, and watch someone else succeed, you know you want to be a part of it. You learn how to do it and feel emboldened to give it a shot.

Modeling behavior means observing the behavior of people you admire, who are often in the same field of expertise or activity as you. Start "local" and look to your parents, family and friends as examples. If you want to be a better sister, then turn to women close to you. Find the people who are best at what they do, then try and emulate them. Social persuasion involves positive reinforcement, coaching and encouragement. Find those people who light the fire inside of you—who make you feel extremely confident. They will provide you with positive feedback, inspiration and motivation.

Live Boldly

I write and speak the words "Live Boldly" frequently. Living boldly is confidently carrying out the plans you set out to accomplish. What you think, say, and do all stems from your confidence. The *Live Boldly* mindset believes that thoughts, words, and actions will lead to a life of helping others feel fulfilled, as well as finding the same fulfillment for yourself. *Live Boldly* is about speaking positive, empowering words over your life and inspiring yourself. It means you accept every challenge as an opportunity to improve and grow stronger. This leads to confidence and self-assurance. This is the path Simone Biles followed in becoming the best women's gymnast in the world.

The 2016 AP Female Athlete of the Year just missed her chance at competing in the 2012 Summer Olympic Games. She had to wait four more years for her shot at gold. She trained hard every day, believing, thinking, and living with a self-improving mindset. She had the 2016 Rio Games in her crosshairs, as she won three consecutive women's all-around world championships. Each competition, each victory made her stronger and more confident. She refused to settle for anything less than gold at all her competitive events. In Rio, her dream came true—four times over. She won the gold medal in four of the five events she competed in. It was a performance for the ages.

When you live boldly—with confidence—life begins to come to you naturally, clearly, and freely. You stop worrying and start living. You achieve a life in harmony and rhythm; one where you exude confidence. Living boldly means living with an open mind and open heart. It requires keen self-awareness, self-control, and an insatiable desire for achieving success.

Obstacles to Living with Confidence

" *The way to develop self-confidence is to do the thing you fear and get a record of successful experiences behind you." — William Jennings Bryan*

- Self-consciousness

- Worry

- Low self-esteem

- Negative or anxious thoughts

- Lack of faith

- Laziness

- Indecision—lack of certainty about direction

Remember, the way we see ourselves is often a mirror reflection of how we see the outside world. While you should always care—to some degree—what others think of you, the most important opinion you should be concerned with is the one you hold of yourself. You have to live with your thoughts and actions each day. Life is much bolder when you're confident in how you approach things. When you find your mind drifting toward doubt, make sure to slow things down.

I had to overcome battles with laziness early on in my career. This was largely because I wasn't doing work that gave meaning to my life. I'm about 86.7 percent more productive when I'm doing what I love (give or take a few *very* unscientific percentage points). When you love what you do, you have passion. Passion leads to enthusiasm. And there is a very strong correlation between enthusiasm and confidence. When we're confident, we live in the moment with joy in our hearts. We stop doubting and worrying.

Another confidence-killer is indecision. Indecision is a dream-crusher that will slow you down. Decisiveness and taking ownership of the circumstances at hand are signs of maturity and wisdom. Decisiveness shows a willingness to rise up and be confident, relying on your ability to overcome fear and find a way to get the job done.

I encourage you always to be kind to yourself. As my friend Amy once told me, "Love yourself like you're your own mother." Focus on thinking positive, building upon the positive feedback you receive, and not dwelling on the negative. Positive thought will give you a greater sense of self-worth and boost your spirits, helping to build your confidence. Then, the sky is the limit to what you can do.

3 Questions on Confidence to Ask Yourself

1. How do you motivate yourself?

2. What are the dominating thoughts of your mind?

3. What words do you say most? Your words and thoughts shape the way you feel about yourself

Value within the Value

❝ *Be humble in your confidence yet courageous in your character."—Melanie Koulouris*

First Impressions

First impressions are sometimes all we have. At least in the eyes of those we aim to influence. Like it or not, this is often the way society chooses to measure and judge us. It's not fair, but it is reality. We see things through the eyes of our experiences and emotions, but others see us through the prism of *their* experiences. When we think further about first impressions, what we're focusing on is presentation, which in and of itself is about confidence. Confidence is the magic potion that we want for ourselves and hope to share with the people we meet—especially the person with whom we wish to spend the rest of our lives.

I have attracted the people I truly desire to have in my life when I have lived with confidence. Confidence is desired in all relationships because it embodies the optimal faith we hope to place in someone. True confidence is not arrogance. It's not braggadocio.

Once, when I was about to go for a job interview, my brother said to me, "You already know another company wants you and is going to make you an offer. Go in with confidence—you're playing with house money!" True confidence is like playing with house money. The concept, of course, comes from gambling—using the money from the casino to fuel and drive future earnings. Remember, Las Vegas wasn't built on winners! But it's the winners who "let it ride" in thought, speech, and action. Those who lead with confidence define the terms for how they wish to live their lives. Playing with house money is a choice made easier, from a psychological standpoint, when we're unafraid of losing anything, even though we would be losing what we just earned. It's a mindset of confidence that soothes anxiety, fear of loss and aversion to risk.

We all have some aversion to risk. We have a natural fear of the unknown and a reluctance toward taking chances. But we find, if we're willing to take a chance, it often pays off handsomely. (Just maybe not always at the Blackjack table!) We're all programmed with a keen sense for survival, something usually taught and cultivated by the wonderful people who raised us. Many of us are given conservative guidance and advice, designed to position us for success and future happiness. Most of the time this is prudent, because it keeps us out of trouble and eliminates potential obstacles from our path.

But too much conservative advice and coaching toward risk aversion can be dangerous. To live is to risk! And to risk is often to take big chances—to make big bets on ourselves. I've come to believe there is no surer bet than the one you place on yourself.

Confident State of Mind

> " If being an egomaniac means I believe in what I do and in my art or music, then in that respect you can call me that ... I believe in what I do, and I'll say it."—John Lennon

I'm not advising against a conservative approach in some areas of life. Often with our finances, for example, we need to stay a conservative course. The same can be said for advising someone recovering from sickness, injury, or depression. But when we really break down our choices and the paths for how our lives can unfold, we can consider the prospect of winning several hands of poker and playing with the "excess" cash that comes our way.

We'll find we've conceived a confident way of thinking that knows no worry, believes with a winner's mindset, and possesses confidence that prepares us to experience happiness and success. Confidence is a state of mind. It's part of our attitude. We can integrate confidence into how we prepare for exams at school, or how we muster up the courage to ask a boy or girl on a date. Confidence goes a long way toward determining where we work, the people with whom we choose to surround ourselves, and the biggest decisions we make in life.

A Story to Tell

> " *Once we believe in ourselves, we can risk curiosity, wonder, spontaneous delight, or any experience that reveals the human spirit."—E. E. Cummings*

Twelve years ago, I was drifting along in a sales job without goals or any plan that would move me forward. I didn't know what I wanted. As a result, I lacked confidence. I was doing too many things I wasn't good at, and not enough of the things I do well. But it was all a learning experience. It was adventurous, frustrating, exciting, and anxious. It was like getting behind the wheel of a Ferrari for the first time and revving it up on the freeway... without control of the brakes.

As I cruised along, I realized that I wasn't in any kind of career—I was ina job. I started to think about going back to graduate school. I needed to learn more skills, plan better for my future, and experience more of life without the pressures of a sales quota. I created my list of schools. I narrowed it down and in the end, after making a long road trip to the South, I fell in love with the University of Georgia. It would be 1,000 miles from home and a completely different way of life. I immediately thought of how much I'd miss my family. But I felt a deep conviction—a bold feeling of confidence—that this was the place for me. As I often do, I decided to trust my intuition. But I still had a few phone calls to make.

For the biggest decisions in life, I've always reached out to my dad, my brothers, and my mom. They have served as my inner circle, lending their voices of experience and wisdom. I'll always remember what my dad said to me, because I thought he'd be against this move.

My dad tends to play things a bit more conservatively. And I did have a scholarship offer on the table from a school closer to home. We hashed out all the pros and cons. My dad gave a long, deep breath. Then he said: *"If you feel that this is what you want, then I'm behind you 100 percent. Go with your heart and be confident."*

These are words I'll hold dear and remember for the rest of my life. In many ways, they've become my mantra for when I make big decisions. Big decisions require time to process all the information. While others can advise or coach us, only we should be the ones who confidently decide what is best for our lives. Only we truly know what is placed in our hearts.

Seek the counsel of others, but make the decision yourself. Once you start to make big decisions for yourself, you grow in confidence. It's an empowering feeling that carries you forward.

Results of Confidence

Confidence comes from repetition, preparation, and faith. It's about knowing your identity, who you are, what your beliefs and values are, and why you're doing what you're doing. When you have a purpose and mission behind your actions, you have less time to worry or question your motives and thoughts. This gives you more time to concentrate on living in the moment, being yourself, and performing at a high level of efficiency.

I used to be really shy in high school and college when it came to meeting girls. I never dated much when I was growing up, so I wasn't really sure what to say to girls. I kept thinking I had to be someone I wasn't. Sound like you? What I came to learn after the fact (of course!) was that I just had to be myself. Once I was good ol' me, I could be more confident and comfortable in my own skin. I didn't need to feel like I was acting on the latest tip from some pick-up artist in *Esquire* magazine. I realized how much this mindset translates to all facets of life.

In the end, what matters most with confidence is that you simply need to be yourself. Live your life and don't worry in the moment whether all the pieces will fall into place in your future. Trust that your life will be a happy and fulfilling one—and it will. The dominating thoughts of your mind are what will become your destiny.

Amy Schumer has told me her self-confidence is derived from how she sees herself, as opposed to the way she is seen by others. It's why she focuses more on the positive feedback that she gets and less on the negative. She uses positive thoughts and words to motivate herself. She would tell you to be proud of the way you're living. What I encourage you to do is to go forth in confidence and watch as the wave of positive thought washes over your life and touches the lives of those you encounter.

Game Plan:

1. Practice "self-coaching" to motivate yourself each day. I'm talking about positive encouragement that reprograms the way you think. Use teachers, friends, family members and colleagues who have helped and guided you, as your role models. Take their example and do the same thing for yourself! Speak positive words over your life and nurture

yourself. The way you treat yourself will become a reflection of how you treat others.

2. Build your confidence by understanding the cycle of self-reliance, experience, social acceptance and results. These things feed off one another. The great Babe Ruth once said, "Don't let the fear of striking out hold you back." Walk forward in confidence and trust that your abilities will carry you far!

Notes

[1] "Confidence," *Merriam-Webster*, https://www.merriam-webster.com/dictionary/confidence (accessed May 4, 2017).

[2] Michael Lardon, M.D., *Finding Your Zone: Ten Core Lessons for Achieving Peak Performance in Sports and Life* (TarcherPerigree, 2008).

[3] Albert Bandura, "Vicarious and Self-reinforcement Processes," in *The Nature of Reinforcement* (New York: Academic Press, Inc., 1971), pp. 228–78. Chapter available at https://www.uky.edu/~eushe2/Bandura/Bandura1971.pdf (accessed April 4, 2017).

II
Heart

CHAPTER 5

Altruism

"Every man must decide whether he will walk in the light of creative altruism or in the darkness of destructive selfishness."

— Dr. Martin Luther King Jr.

DEFINITION:

"Unselfish regard for or devotion to the welfare of others" [1]

On the morning of September 11, 2001, Welles Crowther was working for the firm Sandler O'Neill and Partners in the South Tower of the World Trade Center, in Lower Manhattan. Only twenty-four years old, Crowther was loving and bold well beyond his years. He had recently graduated from Boston College, where he played lacrosse and was a beloved member of the community. He set out to earn a living as an equities trader, hoping eventually to have a family and spend his free time as a volunteer fireman.

Eight years earlier, at the age of sixteen, Crowther had become a volunteer firefighter, following in his father's footsteps. He worked alongside his dad for the Empire Hook and Ladder Company in Nyack, New York, his hometown just thirty miles north of the World Trade Center. From the time he was a boy, Crowther had big dreams. He cared deeply about his family and friends. He was the kind of person you wanted in the proverbial foxhole with you when everything went wrong. At such a young age, that was exactly the position Crowther was thrust into on the fateful morning of September 11.

As he started his work day, on the 104th floor of the South Tower, it seemed to be a late summer morning like any other in the big city—beautiful and sunny with limitless possibilities. Suddenly, all of that changed. At 8:46 a large commercial airliner crashed into the North Tower, right next to the building Crowther worked in. Chaos and commotion ensued. Seventeen minutes later, at 9:03, a second plane struck the South Tower less than twenty floors below where Crowther was working.

How could anyone prepare for a moment of this magnitude?

During this time of crisis, Crowther didn't think selfishly of how to save himself. He first called his mother to let her know that he was all right. Then he sprang into action, moving with the type of courage reserved for only the greatest of heroes, sprinting and hustling to save the lives of co-workers and perfect strangers. This was the mindset of a college athlete. A fireman. A winner, who was unwilling to leave anyone behind.

Crowther took charge of an impossible-to-handle situation. He put out fires on floors, administered first aid, and rescued those in need. He helped many individuals get out of the South Tower alive. He turned around and went back inside the burning building several times, rescuing and saving the lives of his fellow New Yorkers. He was last seen heading into the South Tower with members of the New York City Fire Department before the Tower collapsed that morning. The motto of the Fire Department of New York (FDNY) is "New York's Bravest." As Crowther fought for his life in a collapsing building amid searing heat and suffocating smoke, he proved himself to be worthy of the FDNY motto. A true leader.

Crowther lost his life while saving the lives of as many as eighteen people on the morning of September 11.[2]

" *People can live 100 years and not have the compassion, the where- withal to do what he did." — Judy Wein, an employee of the South Tower whose life Crowther saved*

He became a beacon of shining hope for a generation to come on what was, by any account, one of the most tragic days in world history. In life, there's always room to redefine the perceptions of who we are—even the words we use every day. That day, Welles Crowther redefined the word altruism. He put the lives of others far above his own. At some point, in a moment that must have felt like an eternity, he made a choice. He chose to give up his life so that others could go home to their wives, husbands, sons, and daughters.

If only a few more of us in society would live our lives with such devotion and love for others, the world would be a greater place. We may never need to give up our life for someone else, but we can certainly put others first every day. It's our choice. Now, when I think of what it means to be a hero, to be truly altruistic, I think of Welles Crowther.

The Core of Altruism

" *The root of happiness is altruism—the wish to be of service to others." — Dalai Lama*

Altruism is the ultimate expression of selflessness. In other words, it's the opposite of egoism. Altruism is a **devotion** to the well-being of other people. Devotion takes concentration, focus, and effort. Devotion is heartwarming sensitivity, in the form of deep thought and action. Devotion is profound dedication "to a cause, enterprise or activity." [3]

Altruism leads to friendship. Friendship enriches our lives, educates us, teaches us to trust, and stimulates our emotions. Friendship provides us with people who endeavor to make our lives better by caring for us, celebrating with us, and supporting us through difficult times. True friendship is guided by devotion and kindness toward one another.

When I think of altruism, I also think of sacrifice. I think of the most touching example of selfless love—giving one's life to save another. This is the commitment our servicemen and women make each day while protecting our freedoms around the globe. I think also of policewomen and men who risk their lives to keep us safe. Their service is voluntary. Though, were it not for them, where would we turn for assurance and protection against terrorism and evil?

I have the good fortune of knowing childhood friends who are New York City police officers, salt-of-the-earth people who are compassionate and empathetic. I've enjoyed the privilege of working side-by-side with Army and Air Force soldiers while working as a management consultant. The mindset of these heroes is to put the interests of others above their own—even risking their lives, if need be. Few of us will know the power behind serving others in this capacity. But having observed it up close I can tell you the reward outweighs the risk. To give is truly better than to receive. We all have the power, the liberty, to serve someone else and make their life better by demonstrating selfless devotion to their needs.

Obstacles to Living with Altruism

- Selfishness

- Arrogance

- Pride

- Ignorance

- Excessive concern for oneself

Think about all the time that you waste. Go ahead, procrastinate a little bit more. See! You just wasted some more time. Now, look at the hours of your day, the days of your week, and the time within each month. How much of that time do you spend thinking about yourself?

It's essential that we first look out for ourselves—therein lies the paradox. We have to first care for ourselves if we want to care for others. But there's always a tipping point. There is a moment we can actively choose to become self-aware enough to lead with a helping heart. If we focus only on ourselves, life tends to become less fulfilling. We are social creatures created to love. If we only look inward, never out, we miss opportunities to make a difference in other people's lives. There needs to be a balance if we desire to live more virtuously and make better use of our time.

We waste time on websites like Twitter becoming followers, on Facebook being fans, all while we could be leaders today. Many of the technological distractions that occupy our time are things that tend to cultivate a selfish prism through which we view the world. A few months ago, I was walking down a side street in Manhattan and I literally bumped into a man—around my age—whose face was buried in his smartphone. The sidewalk was so narrow, I didn't even have time to move, and right before we collided I yelled, "EXCUSE ME!"

He didn't hear me. We bumped into one another, and his glasses went flying. So did a few unsavory four-letter words aimed in my direction. I must have delayed his tweet.

Of course, he committed no crime. "Reckless use of a smartphone" is not a prosecutable offense. There was no citizen's arrest to be made that day! But he was completely consumed by a device that was doing no good to anyone. Technology has helped our society in remarkable ways. It has also done a lot to take away from our ability to serve one another. We've become more isolated and insulated in our own bubbles of self-absorption.

The worst mistakes we can make in life are thinking that other people don't care what we have to say, and that we can't offer value through our unique contributions. In my work consulting with business leaders and senior government professionals, I've realized that everyone has an immense amount to contribute to humanity. We can make a positive difference in the world simply by activating our talents and following through with faith and persistence. When we do this for others, we are operating with the mindset of a servant leader. There's no pride or selfishness in that.

Value within the Value

" *When you are able to shift your inner awareness to how you can serve others, and when you make this the central focus of your life, you will then be in a position to know true miracles in your progress toward prosperity." — Wayne Dyer*

It's human nature to think first of your needs—and your family's—for survival and safety. No one should ever begrudge you that. Once you have established these securities, however, I encourage you to think of putting others first, starting with the way you plan your day. What good is all the money, fame, or creature comforts in the world if you have no one to share them with? Time is of immense value. Time in solitude, alone with ourselves for introspection and contemplation, is time very well spent. But what about the time we share with others? That is when we should immerse ourselves in the moment and add joy to people's lives.

We should want to create the best "user experience" that we can for the people we invite into our lives. That involves thinking of their needs, comforts, and desires. It requires that we take time to know people better, even when they're the ones closest to us. People change. We all mature into adults with changed views of ourselves and the world around us. The greatest way to continue to evolve in our own right is to show an active interest in others through listening, empathy, and helping to build the community around us.

Lessons in Servant Leadership

> *Embracing our vulnerabilities is risky but not nearly as dangerous as giving up on love and belonging and joy—the experiences that make us the most vulnerable. Only when we are brave enough to explore the darkness will we discover the infinite power of our light."* [4] *—Brené Brown*

For our relationships to thrive, each of us needs to begin with an open extension of empathy. Empathy must be genuine and heartfelt—otherwise, everyone will know they're dealing with a phony. To show you care, you have to want to get to know others. Being a servant leader means putting the interests of others above your own. Don't let the fear of doing this hold you back! If you're afraid to be vulnerable, ditch that fear. Vulnerability is one of the greatest traits you can develop.

I recently met a successful businessman for a cup of coffee on a Saturday afternoon. He said some golden words to me. They meant that much more because he met me in an effort to help me out:

"I make every effort to give without expecting anything in return."

Wouldn't the world be a beautiful place if everyone not only thought that way—but acted on it? Yet it seems, in my experience, the people who behave this way really stand out. They're memorable, because they're few and far between. Far too often, we act purely in our own interest. We have to "make it" first and do things our way—which usually means "getting ours" and not caring for what others get. We take advantage of the generous help of others without giving in return.

Eventually, that comes back to bite us. I've been on both sides. As a millennial and businessman, I've relied on the help of others in my personal and professional network. I've met some extraordinarily generous people who have advised, coached, and mentored me. I've chosen to return the favor and give without the expectation of any reward.

" *Good leaders must first become good servants." – Robert Greenleaf*

The benevolence of these mentors has helped me as I've carved out a career for myself. I am nothing today without the people who have had my back and looked out for me. Some of these people were new acquaintances that simply cared and wanted to help. Think about that: on the surface, it would seem there was nothing in it for them. They were helping to better my situation. Yet, as the saying goes, it is far better to give than to receive. There is a very powerful feeling of self-satisfaction that comes from helping others. When I help others, I receive gratitude and respect from people who are willing to help me grow as a writer, or tell others of my goodwill. I gain colleagues and acquaintances that make the transition from stranger to friend.

3 Questions on Altruism to Ask Yourself

1. What are the causes that motivate you?

2. Who are the people you want to help?

3.   Are you willing to put others before yourself?

I met with a marketing executive recently who said to me, "The way I show up, is how others show up." This is the ultimate "Lead by Example" mantra (as opposed to leading only with words). As the saying goes, "Actions speak louder than words."

I encourage you to think about the way you feel throughout your day, to meditate on those thoughts and make sense of where you derive satisfaction. We all get down. There is frustration that comes with living in our modern world and sometimes feeling like our voice is not heard. We all want to feel motivated to do good. We seek gratification through the work we do, the people we interact with, and the activities that inspire us. I encourage you to harness your energy toward service. Generate excitement from doing good to help others in need. You'll be truly amazed at how much this will positively influence your life and outlook.

Results of Altruism

The results of practicing altruism are a lifetime of fulfillment and peace of mind. While you may not always see it in your day-to-day life, you can be assured that you made the world a better place. Welles Crowther sadly did not live to see the results of his heroism and altruism on the morning of September 11, but his actions had an impact on the lives of thousands of people. The people he saved have families who are eternally grateful for him. His name will live on forever in the pages of this book, at the 9/11 Memorial in Lower Manhattan, in honor at sporting events, firehouses, and wherever heroes are praised.

I count myself as an indirect beneficiary of Mr. Crowther's actions. My life is richer for knowing his story. Chances are, your life is richer for knowing someone who lives selflessly and genuinely cares about the positive impact their actions have on your life. You may know the true meaning of love thanks to someone who gave you everything they had and never expected anything in return.

I think of my mother and father. When I was younger, I thought my mom and dad were heroes. I think for any of us who've had great parents, we feel this way. My parents always let me know that they loved me. They told me, they demonstrated it through their actions, and they showed the most genuine, selfless care for me, which was always rooted in devotion to my best interests.

They provided me with a foundation of values and morals that were passed down from the way their parents raised them. I've benefited tremendously from two great brothers, who took the time to teach me how to play basketball, introduce me to great music, and let me know right from wrong. Those things take time. They take love and care. I'm thankful to my family and grateful each day for growing up around people who devoted themselves to making my life a better one.

Take the time to thank the people who have helped you along the way. Then, return the favor to the people whose lives you touch. Hopefully, you will have the good fortune of both giving and receiving with a generous heart.

Game Plan:

1. Start planning your week. From there, let it trickle down to planning tasks for your day. I use categories like, Family, Job, Personal Development and Health & Wellness, to help me determine how I want to win each week. The better planned and prepared you are for all that comes your way, the more time you'll have to serve others.

2. Create a list of the family, co-workers, fellow students, and friends in your life. In a few sentences, write out the impact you've had on their life, as well as the impact they've had on yours. How often do you tell the people you care about that you love and appreciate them? We all spend countless hours on our electronic devices. Chances are, it may only take you a few seconds to send a text message. Why not take a few seconds right now to tell your mom, dad, brother, sister, or friend that you're thinking of them? They'll appreciate it. And you'll feel better.

3. Make a commitment to serve one person this week without any selfish motivation. As you plan your week, write the name of the person—and the action—into your plan. Dedicate yourself!

Notes

[1] "Altruism," *Merriam-Webster*,
https://www.merriam-webster.com/dictionary/altruism (accessed March 19, 2017).

[2] Watch "The Man in the Red Bandana," ESPN, available at http://www.espn.com/video/clip?id=11505494 (accessed April 3, 2017).

[3] Merriam Webster

[4] Brené Brown, *The Gifts of Imperfection: Let Go of Who You Think You're Supposed to Be and Embrace Who You Are* (Center City, MN: Hazelden, 2010), 6. See the rest of Brené Brown's work at http://brenebrown.com/ (accessed April 3, 2017).

CHAPTER 6

Kindness

"Kindness is the language which the deaf can hear and the blind can see."

—*Mark Twain*

<u>DEFINITION:</u>

Kind: "Having or showing a gentle nature and a desire to help others: wanting and liking to do good things and to bring happiness to others."[1]

Raising three boisterous boys in a two-bedroom apartment and maintaining her sanity is my mom's biggest accomplishment. I look back and marvel at all she did for us. She provided us with the values that have shaped us into the men we are today. We were fortunate to attend great public schools growing up, but the best education we received came within the walls of Apartment F4.

My mom was the central planner and organizer for our lives. Cooking? Check. Cleaning? Check. Getting us ready for school? Check. Driving us to countless sporting events, friends' houses and doctor appointments? Check. Playing referee between all our indoor football games and brotherly fights? Oh, yeah. You didn't mess with mom! My mother put all of us first and did so out of the kindness and love in her heart. These lessons were passed down to her from her mother and father, a virtuous cycle of giving—one I now try to share with my family.

As I matured, I thought of how my mom never complained about the responsibility. She made it look easy. She put stickers on our brown-bag lunches and wrote us notes in those lunch bags. She always remembered us on our birthdays and holidays, letting us know how special and loved we are. My mom has always had kindness down to an art form. She still sends me cards on Valentine's Day and St. Patrick's Day. My mom keeps Hallmark in business. She's like the Maya Angelou of greeting cards. Her lessons show that kindness is the gift that keeps on giving. It's infectious and full of love and empathy.

When we're touched by kind acts, we find a natural desire to return the favor. It's like one big game of "pay it forward." We don't necessarily need to pick up the Caramel Macchiato frappe for the person behind us at Starbucks (but if you see me, get me the Venti!). Kindness doesn't need to be monetary. We can add love and happiness to someone's day with a simple smile. We can volunteer our time at a community center to help disadvantaged youth. The possibilities of sharing our talents and time with others are endless.

I may never be able to pay my mom back for how kind and good she's been to me. But I can pay it forward to my family and community. You can, too.

The Core of Kindness

> " *Nobody cares how much you know, until they know how much you care."—Theodore Roosevelt*

Kind people are those who leave an indelible mark on our lives. They're the people we tend to remember. We identify with kindness, in part, because it is synonymous with "The Golden Rule." We want to be treated kindly, so we strive to treat our fellow men and women this way. Kindness leads to sincerity, empathy, and curiosity. It spawns a desire to seek these qualities in people we meet, even if we won't reap any material gain in the "transaction." That is exactly where I would like to take this discussion on kindness.

Kindness is not a transaction! You can't outbid *superboy2485* on eBay for kindness, as if it were perfume or galoshes. Though, we could all use a nice pair of galoshes! Kindness is a transformative builder of relationships. It influences our way of thinking. It impacts how we treat friends, colleagues, family members and perfect strangers. Kindness is warm, inviting, other-seeking, and it pursues friendship and good in others.

Kindness is a testament to our inner DNA: it affords us the opportunity to show the outside world the goodwill in our hearts. Kindness is the cousin of respect. (The good kind of cousin—you know, the one you *actually* get along with.) Treating people with kindness demonstrates a form of respect. When you are kind, you immediately open yourself up to an abundance of new conversations, opportunities, and friendships. People want to be a part of kindness—even those of us who are introverted and less likely to initiate conversation. Every one of us desires to be treated kindly.

Kindness could be giving of your time, talent, and treasure to help people in need. Maybe there is a cause that moves you, or there is someone in your life who could use your help today. You may not have the financial resources, but you probably have the time. It is often the things we do first with kindness and love that lead to our boldest opportunities.

Every task or action I've performed in my professional career, I've done both for free and been paid to do. I've been paid to write, and I've written for free. I've been paid to coach basketball, and I've also done so free of charge. I've built a career coaching business from scratch that started out as a hobby (helping friends, neighbors, and co-workers) and became something bigger. My mindset hasn't changed for either.

Give away time to help others. By doing so, you reap marvelous rewards. There are powers you and I may never have on this earth, but the power to change someone's life for the better is always within our reach. It may just be a smile. It could be giving up your seat on the downtown "2" train for an elderly man with achy knees. Maybe it's rescuing the neighbor's young daughter from the middle of the road while a gas-guzzling SUV barrels down the block.

Kindness is a choice you can make every day with the intelligent mind you've been given.

Obstacles to Living with Kindness

- Pride (ego)

- Anger

- Self-absorbed behavior

- Lack of compassion

By treating others with respect and kindness, we earn respect in return. But what about when we let ego or pride get in the way? We become selfish. We start focusing on outcomes that only benefit us. We're far less likely to practice kindness. When you think about it, a lack of kindness is a form of disrespect to ourselves and those around us. The willingness to be kind to others in thought, speech, and action produces goodness that brings blessings to the lives of those we touch. In turn, this comes back to us as a reciprocal gift, which makes this value come full circle.

We add unnecessary suffering to our lives when we only think about meeting our needs. Pride comes before the fall, and fall you will, if all your actions are rooted in a desire to please yourself. How far have you gotten when you've put on blinders and failed to acknowledge others? Or worse yet, when you've been mean to friends, family, or strangers? I don't know about you, but that wars against my soul. It's so much more invigorating to treat people with kindness.

As daughters, sons, sisters, brothers, and parents, we bring greater harmony to our lives by showing kindness to our loved ones. This kindness enriches their lives. It's full of compassion, empathy, and understanding. Is there a cranky uncle or unhappy schoolmate or co-worker in your life? Take one minute out of your day and say something nice to that person. If you can, buy them a coffee. Show people you care—don't just tell them. Make this a priority in your relationships.

Just remember—kindness works both ways. We're best when we lead from the heart, practicing kindness toward others and ourselves. Despite the winds of change and emotion, it's imperative to find time to be kind to yourself. Surround yourself with people who love and empathize with you. This will influence the way you think and behave.

Unleash this power of kindness on the world around you. Kindness is the gift that keeps on giving.

3 Questions on Kindness to Ask Yourself:

1. What are the values that stand out about the people you respect and admire?

2. Why do you feel a wave of positive emotions when you think about them?

3. What things do they say and do that endear them to you?

Value within the Value

" *Kindness in words creates confidence. Kindness in thinking creates profoundness. Kindness in giving creates love." — Lao Tzu*

A Story to Tell

In 2015, I attended a training course offered by my company. The course focused on the successful facilitation of leadership workshops. At the beginning of the training, the two course instructors reviewed the "rules of the road" for the course. At the end of this review, one of the instructors made sure to mention something so simple, yet necessary. He said one of the key points at the start of each facilitation is the choice to say two simple words: "Be Kind."

The reason for this, he went on to add, was that in previous courses that he facilitated, people were often rude to one another. Negative attitudes, as well as pride and ego, got in the way, making things uncomfortable. Maybe you've been there in a school or office setting, watching people scream over one another. It's tough to watch! There are no good manners to be found. Then, someone may even take the last donut from the breakfast table. Come on! Simple kindness is a matter of common decency. Think about it this way:

Why in the world would we not treat one another with kindness?

The world we create around us is boundless and infinite when we are kind, and when we put others first. Generously tip at restaurants. Smile. Open doors for people at the grocery store or deli. Do the "little things," like letting someone into your lane during rush hour traffic. Give sincere handshakes and make eye contact with people. These little things leave people feeling a little bit better about their day, and speak volumes of your character.

Like anyone in rush hour traffic or deprived of sleep, I let anger and frustration get the better of me at times. Then I think about how treating others with disrespect was never in my plans. In truth, doing so always makes me feel far worse, I imagine, than the person on the receiving end of my rant or rude look. It's perspective—always— which helps us witness this truth.

Kindness is the most underrated of all values. I say this, because it's so easy to put our interests, motives, and pursuits first, rather than focusing on our family, friends, or even perfect strangers. The path of least resistance is to live a life centered on ourselves. Life is much richer, much bolder, when we learn and choose to put others first.

Givers and Takers

66 *Carry out a random act of kindness, with no expectation of reward, safe in the knowledge that one day someone might do the same for you." — Princess Diana*

Think about the givers and takers in society. A taker will borrow your car, run their errands, and return the keys—with an empty tank. A giver will allow you to borrow their car and let you return it "whenever is good for you." Takers are transactional people who put themselves first. They'll take your idea for a new social media app and try making it their own, while giving you none of the credit (#notcool). Givers allow your idea to flourish and present you with new opportunities to turn it into a reality.

Taking is the quintessential short-term mindset. And a deceiving one, at that. Ask yourself, when you've been a taker (we all have), have you really ended up better off? Taking is perfectly fine, **as long as we seek to return** the gift in the form of a kind gesture. It is human nature to think of our needs first. It's not wrong if you do. It takes some fine-tuning to see that when we act only as takers, we end up with little of what we want in return. A taker's mentality demonstrates a lack of self-awareness. It's inherently selfish.

Whether people tell you or not, they want to be a part of a giver's relationship of reciprocal value.

When it comes to social and business interactions, those of us who act with kindness receive opportunities and sincere gratitude in return. This is what the takers will never understand, unless they make a significant course correction. Kind people behave like a servant leader—someone who looks to put others' needs before their own. Is this for everyone? You bet it is. We find the ethos and values-based structure of why we do what we do, is one of living for and serving others.

The People We Admire

" *Never believe that a few caring people can't change the world. For, indeed, that's all who ever have."—Margaret Mead*

I admire Ellen DeGeneres because she acts with kindness toward everyone she meets. She does so many nice things for perfect strangers, because she has a heart of gold and wants to leave the world better off. When you tune in to her daytime talk show, she always seems to give a family money for a new house or a scholarship for a child to attend school. Those are powerful acts of kindness that are made possible by a caring mindset focused on serving others. I've found myself deeply touched by her actions. She'd likely remain famous if she only acted in her self-interest. But we know her today for her benevolence and kindness toward everyone. The way she uses her platform as a celebrity to love and care about others is inspiring.

Ellen DeGeneres cares. We want others to care. This is why Facebook is a multi-billion-dollar enterprise. It's why we flock to Twitter and Instagram to see who liked our status, and why we want to share our thoughts with audiences larger than our partners and dogs. My dog is willing to listen, but she's not as empathetic as you might think. Fortunately, you are!

> " *How people treat you is their karma; how you react is yours.* "— *Wayne Dyer*

Because of smartphones, devices, and social media, many of us are conditioned to promote ourselves and look out only for our own best interest, with very little regard for others. It's no surprise that when we enter the proverbial marketplace with our ideas or needs, we're aiming to find a partner who can give us something—while we provide nothing in return! The problem is, the world does not work that way.

It is as simple as citing the law of supply and demand, but it goes even further into the impulses and emotions of the human psyche. Inherently, we were created to love. We are drawn toward generosity, altruism, and kind acts that make the lives of others better. When we sense this moral code is being violated, either against us or against someone else, we get upset. It's aggravating and disappointing to see. For those of us who seek good, we want to return the favor to those who help us. At best, we want to give without expecting anything in return.

Kindness given is kindness received. This is the spirit of caring and the law of reciprocity!

Results of Kindness

"100% Customer Satisfaction"

You've probably seen this advertising slogan before. A guarantee. It sounds great, but these words ring hollow when they're not followed by action. Like a lot of words in advertising, it's best to turn to our Latin: *caveat emptor*, let the buyer beware. What exactly does this mean for our lives? Our personal "customer satisfaction" is peace of mind and heart that comes from being content in our life's work. This means living with love and spending time with people we care about.

Our gift of customer satisfaction to others is the Golden Rule: Do unto others as you would have them do to you. This takes effort. It takes kindness and intention to be nice to someone and to want to help them. The saying, "It takes just a few muscles to frown but many more to smile," is a literal and figurative illustration of the effort required to bring joy to others. If you do the "little things" and view life from the perspective of others, you will deliver the customer satisfaction that guarantees a smile.

“ *Three things in human life are important. The first is to be kind. The second is to be kind. And the third is to be kind."—Henry James*

I think of all the obstacles that stand in our way each day. We face battles and adversity that can get us down if we let them. I think of selfishness, pain, and frustration—and that's only on my morning commute! In all seriousness, there are plenty of reasons why we sometimes get angry or frustrated. It can become easy not to care for others because we're too busy worrying about ourselves.

How do you feel when someone treats you like garbage? Don't worry, that question is rhetorical! We all feel terrible when we are disrespected and even violated. Would you still feel that way if others showed you care, love, and respect? Again, I think we know the answer. Think of how everyone around you would feel if you acted with kindness, first. Or if you decided to care and love, instead of reciprocating hurtful actions. Be kind to those around you. Watch how radically your life begins to change. After all, the simple act of being kind does boost your happiness—even if slightly. Don't just take my word for it. Read the words of University of Oxford scientist, Dr. Oliver Scott Curry:

"People do indeed derive satisfaction from helping others. This is probably because we genuinely care about others' welfare, and because random acts of kindness are a good way of making new friends, and kick-starting supportive social relationships."[2]

Game Plan

1. Think about what matters most to the people in your life. What do they care about—what makes them happy? Ask them! Start showing people you care by taking an active interest in what is most important to them. Kindness is a choice you can make each day.

2. Identify relationships that you can improve. Get to know your bus driver. Invite your co-worker out to lunch. Give a call or send a Facebook message to that old high school buddy you've been on the fence about reaching back to. What are

you waiting for? Be willing to take the first step in showing kindness to someone else.

3. Look people in the eye. Find something nice to say. Start to align your behavior with what benefits the lives of others. Once you change your behavior, start measuring the way your emotions and feelings change. Write down your thoughts. Express to a friend or family member how you feel when you do something that makes someone else's day. Look back on those things and recognize you've taken a step forward. Positive energy breeds positive emotions, which lead to positive actions.

Notes

[1] "Kind," *Merriam-Webster* Learner's Dictionary, http://www.learnersdictionary.com/definition/kind (accessed May 30, 2017).

[2] Dr. Oliver Scott Curry, "Happy to Help? A review of the causes and consequences of kindness," quoted in "Being kind to others does make you 'slightly happier,'" University of Oxford, http://www.ox.ac.uk/news/2016-10-05-being-kind-others-does-make-you-slightly-happier (accessed May 30, 2017).

CHAPTER 7

Gratitude

*"I would maintain that thanks are the highest form of
thought; and that gratitude is happiness doubled by wonder."*

—*G.K. Chesterton*

DEFINITION:

The state of being grateful; thankfulness.[1]

Grateful: Appreciative of benefits received [2]

Few people will ever know what it feels like to be the best in the world at their craft. Even fewer will forgo the opportunity to find out. Bill Havens[3] was a man who knew precisely what it meant to sacrifice an opportunity for a chance at stardom. He had good reason. He wanted to be by his wife's side to watch his second child enter the world.

In 1924, Olympians were the most heralded athletes in the world. Bill Havens was the best canoeist. He was undefeated in all previous paddling competitions and was regarded as the favorite to win the gold medal at the Summer Olympic Games in Paris. Havens was dominant. The Olympics were his opportunity to show the world just how great he was.

During training for the Olympics, Havens found out that his wife was pregnant. Great news! There was just one small wrinkle. His son was due to arrive right around the time of the Olympic Games. Bill Havens had a very big decision to make. Should he continue the pursuit of his dream or stay at home with his wife to support her during this very special time?

In those days, it took nine days to travel by ship from the United States to Europe. Havens couldn't just travel to the event, compete, and jet home in hopes that he'd arrive in time for his son's birth. It was go or not go. Family or dream first. The Olympics provided the platform for Havens to deliver a record-setting performance in front of a global audience. This was his time to memorialize a moment he had surely envisioned many times in his dreams. Except, it wasn't to be. Bill Havens decided to pass up the opportunity. He stayed home.

His brother, Bud, who was also a member of the U.S. rowing team, took his place. Bud went on to win four medals (three gold). Four days after the paddling events had ended, Bill Havens' second child, Frank, was born. He was a father for the second time. Over the years and decades to come, Bill Havens' two sons, Frank and Bill Jr., would go on to become world-class canoers who competed in national events representing their country.

Frank Havens won a silver medal at the 1948 Olympic Games in London. But his sights were on gold. He trained harder. Four years later, at the Olympic Games in Helsinki, Finland, Frank Havens was the favorite to win gold. Rarely do moments like this come along for one person, let alone the son of a man who chose to pass on his chance at greatness. It was redemption time for the Havens family.

The gold medal that had eluded Bill Havens, due to his act of love, went to his son Frank twenty-eight years later. Frank reached the pinnacle of his sport. Prior to his return to the United States to share his success with his family, he realized there was one thing he wanted to do: pen a letter to his father. All throughout his time at those Helsinki Games, Frank thought of his father—the man who gave up a likely gold medal to be there for his birth. Here is the letter Frank wrote his father:

Dear Dad,

Thanks for waiting around for me to get born in 1924. I'm coming home with the gold medal you should have won.

Your loving son,

Frank

We may never be able to repay those who grace us with benevolent acts of kindness and goodwill. And often we struggle to find the spoken words. Frank Havens shared a special bond with his father. He was gracious enough to recognize how special his moment was, and the depth of gratitude he felt for his father. He took the time to write a heartfelt letter. A simple expression of gratitude can change a life. "Thanks" endure forever in the hearts and minds of those who both give and receive.

The Core of Gratitude

" *Gratitude turns what we have into enough, and more. It turns denial into acceptance, chaos into order, confusion into clarity ... it makes sense of our past, brings peace for today, and creates a vision for tomorrow."* — *Melody Beattie*

It's beneficial for your well-being to take the time to realize all the good things that you have in your life. I practice gratitude every day, giving thanks to God, my family and those who have created opportunities for me to be happy and successful. I find that it makes me a much more positive person. It adds light and energy to my day. Have you thought about this? Do you find yourself giving thanks? If you do, I think you'll find that gratitude leads to a positive way of thinking.

Dr. Melanie Greenberg, author of *The Stress-Proof Brain*, writes in *Psychology Today*:

Feeling and expressing gratitude turns our mental focus to the positive, which compensates for our brains' natural tendency to focus on threats, worries, and negative aspects of life. As such, gratitude creates positive emotions like joy, love, and contentment which research shows can undo the grip of negative emotions like anxiety. Fostering gratitude can also broaden your thinking, and create positive cycles of thinking and behaving in healthy, positive ways.[4]

When something good happens in your life, be thankful. Be grateful that you get to live each day with purpose and the opportunity to create your own destiny. It's easy to turn negative or blame people when things don't go our way. God knows I've done it plenty of times, and my hunch is that you could say the same. But where has that ever led us? Certainly, not to happiness or peace of mind. When we turn negative, we're not thankful for the good things we have. Because we cannot make sense of things, we turn to doubt, which is never helpful.

These are precisely the moments where we need to turn the negative into positive and express thanksgiving, not rejection. While there will be grief, unrest, and suffering in life, which deserve their time of mourning, it's best to recognize these moments for what they are: moments. They're not enduring periods of hurt. All it takes sometimes is a look around to realize how blessed and fortunate we are to have this gift of life and wonderful people to share it with. It's the classic glass half-empty, glass half-full analogy. We can dwell on things that drag us down, or use gratitude to help us appreciate all that is good in our worlds. Then, we'll never be down for long.

Obstacles to Living with Gratitude

- Selfishness

- Pride

- Unwillingness to praise others

We lose a lot of energy and we end up hurting ourselves by living and brooding in negative emotions. It's simply not an easy way to live. We all spend time talking about nagging, trivial, and insignificant things. We all complain a lot. All right, I'll speak for myself: I know I do! Maybe it helps to take a load off sometimes, but too much is unhealthy. Why not focus on being grateful for what we have and for the people we love? Our aim should be to eliminate all outward anxiety and show our inner emotions of love, happiness, and enjoyment of company.

When we're with the people we care about most—or even when we're on our own, focusing on our lives—we should be mindful of how precious life's moments are. Rich or poor, during moments of distress or joy, we have a lot to be thankful for. Selfishness is what makes us hold in our expressions of gratitude and hide them from view. Instead of showing appreciation to a colleague and telling her she did a great job on her presentation, we may fall into the foolish trap of thinking a demonstration of admiration shows inferiority. Once again, pride tends to rear its ugly head as a major obstacle to living a life with values.

If you're afraid about showing vulnerability, know this: The act of giving thanks and showing gratitude toward someone else will come back to you in a reward of great abundance. You'll feel better, you'll gain the respect of others, and people will want to return the favor to you. Foolish pride is a zero-sum game. You will lose. Don't give in to your lesser nature. Give thanks, instead.

Value within the Value

66 *When we focus on our gratitude, the tide of disappointment goes out, and the tide of love rushes in."—Kristin Armstrong*

I'm willing to bet you have more needs in your life that are met than you think. I urge you to live with an abundance mindset, one that recognizes good graces and understands the difference between luxuries and necessities. You see, the negative emotions tend to creep in when we think that luxuries or non-essential "good-to-have's" are actual needs. Abraham Maslow's hierarchy of needs, which focuses on physiological and safety concerns first, illuminates what true needs really are.

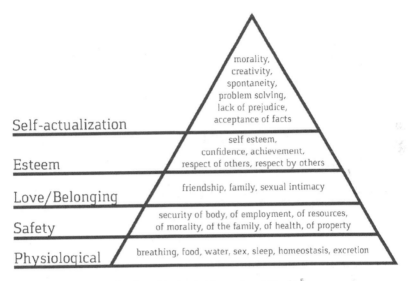

Abraham Maslow's Hierarchy of Needs [5]

Many of us take for granted the roofs over our heads, which provide us shelter and safety. We usually don't think about the simple fact that we're protected from the elements and spared the hardship of living each day with worry of whether we'll survive! This is a call to appreciate the simple things in life. Maybe, like me, you've traveled this country or the world and spoken with people who live each day wondering when—or if—their next meal will arrive. In Western society, it seems our biggest concern, at times, is whether the mobile data reception on our iPhone will fade on our car ride to the movies.

If you're fortunate enough to have access to a mobile phone or laptop computer, chances are your most basic needs are met. You may in fact be blessed enough to come from a loving family, or to have a partner who cherishes you and adds value to your life. This gives you a greater sense of self-worth in who you are.

If we want reward that comes from happiness, peace of mind, and self-satisfaction, we must give and say, "Thank you." Gratitude is a form of humility and kindness, which is a language received with openness by anyone with a compassionate heart. Showing thanks is acknowledging good on the part of another human being. It's paying a compliment and a nod to someone else's attitude and effort.

You will always win and further yourself when you thank those who lift your spirit. It's a necessity for the person who seeks to find greater harmony with God and others. But don't just do it for others. Do it for yourself. You'll live a happier life. And when you have time to reflect on your current lot in life, you'll understand the power of being thankful for what you have.

Gratitude helps keep us humble, respectful, and open to living with stronger faith and joy. It truly centers us in our relationships, in our thoughts, and in how we make sense of our lives. Many of us are blessed to express who we are and to pursue our dreams. Dwell and meditate on how fortunate you are the next time you grow angry and turn sour. Look around you. Take a walk outside, spend some time in solitude and change your perspective on how you view your world. You'll thank yourself. And you can thank me, later.

3 Questions on Gratitude to Ask Yourself:

1. Do you let people know how thankful you are for their presence in your life?

2. Do you take time each day to express gratitude for the life you have?

3. Do you know people who always express their thanks for the life they have? Emulate these people.

A Story to Tell

In my hometown, there's a man everyone knows by name. His name is José, and he's been running his barber shop for nearly fifty years. He's a hometown legend, a crafty barber, and one of the nicest men you'll ever meet. These days, it's hard to find barber shops where everything is done to precision. At José's shop you can get an old-fashioned shave, and after your hair has been exquisitely trimmed and groomed, you leave with chills down your spine. Maybe that's from the after-shave lotion and the talcum powder. I like to think it's the magical feeling of being in the presence of a special man.

José fled communist Cuba in the early 1960s, after Fidel Castro came to power. He left behind his family, loved ones, and his youth. He left behind ... everything. When he touched down on U.S. soil, he wasn't looking for any hand-outs. He never wanted pity or to blame others for his misfortune. He looked forward, rather than looking back. He's never taken a single day for granted. He says the best day of his life is when he became a U.S. citizen. He has a heartfelt appreciation for the opportunity he was given. Despite his warmth, love, and deep faith, more than any other value, José's life is a testament to being grateful for all that he has.

Each time I see him, whether it's going in for a haircut or passing by to say hello, I ask him how he's doing. He replies, "Doing well, thank God." He's a deeply religious man who always gives thanks to God. His words are steeped in gratitude toward his customers and for each day he lives and simply gets to do the job he loves. He's grateful his life has unfolded the way it has. So am I. He's a pillar of the community and an example of how to live with joy, love, and gratitude in our hearts.

Results of Gratitude

> " *Thankfulness is the beginning of gratitude. Gratitude is the completion of thankfulness. Thankfulness may consist merely of words. Gratitude is shown in acts." —Henri Frederic Amiel*

Dr. Robert Emmons, a professor of psychology at UC-Davis, has extensively studied the science of gratitude. He is a leading expert in the field. He lists powerful benefits of gratitude, breaking down the value by physical, psychological and social benefits:

Physical

- Stronger immune systems

- Less bothered by aches and pains

- Lower blood pressure

- Exercise more and take better care of their health

- Sleep longer and feel more refreshed upon waking

Psychological

- Higher levels of positive emotions

- More alert, alive, and awake

- More joy and pleasure

- More optimism and happiness

Social

- More helpful, generous, and compassionate

- More forgiving

- More outgoing

- Feel less lonely and isolated[6]

We see that practicing gratitude adds tremendous value to our lives in many ways. These results are the benefits of showing sincere appreciation and thanks for what we have. Gratitude leads to optimism. We find ourselves living with greater anticipation and a futuristic mindset that embraces new opportunities, as well as change. Each day becomes one that we look forward to more, with a renewal in self-awareness and compassion. We come to live the life we've always wanted.

As I've matured, I've continued to pursue my dreams. But now, my dreams aren't just about me and what I want to accomplish. I dream about watching my son fulfill his own dreams one day. I'm grateful every day that I have such a wonderful boy. I've been blessed with such a special family. With each passing day, it becomes clearer just how grateful I am for all I have.

Think about your family. Maybe, it's not your parents or siblings. It could be relatives or dear friends. It may be your co-workers. Find your family. Tell them that you love them. Tell them you're thankful to have them in your life. Let gratitude shine new light on your life and watch as it illuminates your surroundings.

Game Plan

1. Using the example of Dr. Emmons' benefits, do some reverse-engineering. Work backwards from the benefits! To reap the benefits, you have to behave in a way that helps you achieve them. The foundation of your behavior is your beliefs, attitude and values-structure. Lead with gratitude. Give thanks for the life you have, even if you're currently struggling through a difficult time. Practice gratitude to shape your mind with positive thoughts and an inspired outlook for the day.

2. What are you most thankful for in your life? People? Opportunities? Material possessions? For the people you are grateful for, do you let them know? Do you return the favor to them, for their kindness, by asking, "How can I help you?" Start saying, "Thank you," more often. Say it after each encounter you have with someone. People will want to return compassion and generosity toward you, if you're always giving it out.

Notes

[1] "Gratitude," *Merriam-Webster*, https://www.merriam-webster.com/dictionary/gratitude (accessed May 16, 2017).

[2] Grateful: Appreciative of benefits received

[3] "Havens Olympic History," TeamUSA, http://www.teamusa.org/~/media/USA_Canoe_Kayak/Documents/Havens%20Leadership%20Award/Havens%20Olympic%20History.pdf (accessed May 16, 2017).

[4] Melanie Greenberg, Ph.D., "How Gratitude Leads to a Happier Life," *Psychology Today*, November 22, 2015, https://www.psychologytoday.com/blog/the-mindful-self-express/201511/how-gratitude-leads-happier-life (accessed May 16, 2017).

[5] J. Finklestein, "Diagram of Maslow's Hierarchy of Needs", October 27, 2006, https://commons.wikimedia.org/wiki/File:Maslow%27s_hierarchy_of_needs.svg (accessed March 20, 2017),via the original work of Dr. Abraham Maslow in his 1954 book, *Motivation and Personality* (Harper & Brothers)

[6] Robert Emmons, Ph.D., "Why Gratitude is Good," University of California Berkeley, Greater Good The Science of a Meaningful Life, November 16, 2010, http://greatergood.berkeley.edu/article/item/why_gratitude_is_good/ (accessed February 21, 2017)

CHAPTER 8

Love

"Love is patient, love is kind. It is not jealous, is not pompous, it is not inflated, it is not rude, it does not seek its own interests, it is not quick-tempered, it does not brood over injury, it does not rejoice over wrongdoing but rejoices with the truth. It bears all things, believes all things, hopes all things, endures all things. Love never fails."

—1 Corinthians 13: 4–8

<u>**DEFINITION:**</u>

(1) Strong affection for another arising out of kinship or personal ties (2) attraction based on sexual desire: affection and tenderness felt by lovers (3) affection based on admiration, benevolence, or common interests [1]

Twenty-eight minutes before midnight, on a clear November evening in 2014, the greatest gift I've ever received came into my life at Lenox Hill Hospital in New York City. For as long as I live, there may never be an experience as vivid, gripping, and powerful as when I saw my son for the first time. I wanted to be a father, and by the grace of God, I was given that opportunity. I couldn't take my eyes off him as he kicked, screamed, and cried in the cutest voice I'd ever heard. This indescribable feeling of love was unlike any I've ever felt. Maybe you know the feeling.

In the nine months leading up to his birth, I attended every doctor appointment my wife had. No exaggeration—every appointment. Through rain, sleet, snow, and cabbie-honking midtown traffic, I was there. I was so excited to be a part of something so special, I wasn't willing to miss a minute. On the morning of his birth, my wife's water broke. Somehow, despite thinking my heart would start racing faster than a Kentucky Derby thoroughbred, I remained calm. We made some lunch, got in the car, and drove to the hospital. Love and a brand-new life awaited us.

Boy, did life change for my family that night. As excited as I was for my son's arrival, I was dreading the lack of sleep ahead. Oh yeah, and that whole changing poopy diapers thing (that my dear friends, is an act of love right there)!

As I became a parent for the first time—a *dad*—I immediately thought of my parents. The truth is, even now, when I hear the word "parent," I still think first of my mother and father. I think about the remarkable, loving model they provided for me and my two brothers. I've learned so much from them about how to be a loving and caring parent. They sacrificed and did everything to make my life one filled with opportunity and love. Now, it's my turn—at all hours of the night and day. Sometimes, at 3:43 a.m. while I'm rocking my son back to sleep, I find myself thinking: *Am I really someone's dad?!* It's an exhilarating feeling.

I want to be there for all the growth, the good times and bad— because there will be bad days—and to be the rock of support for him that my mom and dad have been for me. I'm a parent, and I've learned how powerful the gift of love is; not just to receive, but to give. I dedicate myself each day to love my son and give him the best life possible. I'm Dad now. Or should I say, from the angelic lips of a 2-year-old, "Da-da."

Author and Son

Whether you're a parent, hope to be one someday, or you're simply the apple of your parents' eye, know that you are loved. Life is a bold journey of love. The power of that love given to you, you will someday give to another person in return. That is the greatest gift of all.

The Core of Love

> " *We need others physically, emotionally, intellectually; we need them if we are to know anything, even ourselves.*" — *C. S. Lewis*

C. S. Lewis' book, *The Four Loves*[2], provides the best framework for love I've ever seen. He uses four Greek words for love: *storge* (affection), *philia* (friendship), *eros* (passionate or romantic love), and *agape*[3] ("the highest form of love, charity; the love of God for man and of man for God"). This foundation sets the tone for how we give and receive love and make sense of what it is. And it's through the words of Lewis that I ask you to view this most important value.

The constant of love is that it's pure and self-giving. Love is complete when we accept the selfless love of others and give love freely to another, without any expectation of return. While it is truly better to give than to receive, it is important that our hearts are open and accepting to love from someone else. Both need to be in place for true love to exist. I felt it made the most sense to clarify love by each type that Lewis sets out in the book. I hope you find this framework and understanding as rewarding as I have.

Friendship

> " *Friendship arises out of mere companionship when two or more of the companions discover that they have in common some insight or interest or even taste which the others do not share and which, till that moment, each believed to be his (or her) own unique treasure (or burden).*" — *C. S. Lewis*

We may not always think of friendship as love, but true friendship is a beautiful bond created in the spirit of love and care for another person. Friendship is shaped in our youth by the children we go to school with, neighbors on our block, or teammates. As we grow, we find these relationships become more loving and caring than the days of playing tag on the playground or soccer at the local park. Friendship adds so much joy and meaning to our lives. We learn from friends, and they likewise learn from us. Many of the values we adopt, as well as our first experiences—like going to school—we share with our friends.

As we become adults, our relationships change, especially with our parents. While we were once their dependents, we become friends who understand each other's needs in a loving, more unique way. We learn what it's like to be a parent (if we have children) and what it means to care for our parents, like they've done for us all our lives. A few years ago, during a stroll at the Long Beach boardwalk on Long Island, my mom told me, "Chris, you'll always be my son. But now that you're a grown-up, you can view me as a friend." It was my Mom's way of telling me: *I'll always have your back. I'll always love you.*

The truth is, my mom has always loved me with her whole heart and soul. It's just that our relationship has evolved. We're best friends now. When we have a friend like that in our lives, we are always in the presence of love.

Affection

> ❝ In my experience, it is affection that creates this taste, teaching us first to notice, then to endure, then to smile at, then to enjoy, and finally to appreciate, the people who 'happen to be there.'" — C. S. Lewis

Affection is like the famous light blue blanket Linus (of *Charlie Brown* fame) carries with him everywhere. It covers us over, soothes us, and makes us feel warm and fuzzy inside. Affection can be the love of a parent toward their newborn baby. It can be that familiar feeling of love we have for our partner, greeting them when they walk in the door from work. But it can also be the feeling we have for people who aren't our loved ones. We may have deep affection for the people in our hometown who remind us of our lives when we were young. It's the feeling—both given and received—that makes us feel good and special. Affection leads us toward another soul and manifests itself into a form of love.

Eros (Romantic Love)

> ❝ The event of falling in love is of such a nature that ... it has over-leaped the massive wall of our selfhood; it has made appetite itself altruistic, tossed personal happiness aside as a triviality and planted the interests of another in the center of our being." – C.S. Lewis

Have you ever been in love? Even if you haven't, you've surely imagined what it must feel like. Both the anticipation of the feeling and the feeling itself are magical. Lewis' wording is so perfect here: "... planted the interests of another in the center of our being." That is what romantic love is: putting our loving partner before ourselves and feeling inspired while we do it. Both the romantic and sexual nature of *Eros* go hand-in-hand. We were created to love, and we were literally created by sexual love—the act of sexual intercourse between a man and a woman. We are sexual creatures. We desire to explore and share this gift with someone special. In *Eros*, our heart leads us, but we need our minds to ground us. The power of *Eros* is enormous, and will take us captive as no other worldly feeling can.

Charity

> " *The loves prove that they are unworthy to take the place of God by the fact that they cannot even remain themselves and do what they promise to do without God's help.*" — *C. S. Lewis*

The last, but not least, of Lewis's four loves is charity, which he believes comes from God (as do I). God created us to love him and one another, and to be loved by him and his people. God places people in our lives for a reason, to help lead, guide, and love us. We're also placed there to lead, guide, and love others. When we choose to love God and our fellow women and men, we draw closer to a destiny that leads us to our purpose in life.

We are meant to find our calling in life. For you, that may be as a loving parent or as a pediatrician who serves young children. Whatever it may be, here, on this road, when we abide in God's love, we will grow in greater love for him and one another. We'll realize the power of selfless devotion. Loving our neighbor multiplies God's love. We all want a more loving, peaceful world, and that begins with us. We can choose to focus just on ourselves, or we can love and live for others, thereby creating the world we envision in our dreams.

Focus all your energy on love. Love your fellow men and women, love yourself and love the life you have. Because when you go "all in" and commit to loving with all you've got, you will find happiness and peace. It's the way God calls us to live.

Obstacles to Living with Love

- Anger

- Envy

- Selfishness

- Greed

- Pride

You will find yourself shining as a beacon of light in this world, when you take the time to love and care for others. We all know people who only pursue their own self-interest with little regard for others. Selfishness is one of the plagues of modern society. It makes our lives feel off-track. When we love and genuinely care for others, we often find the favor returned to us in even greater measure. There's a reason why unselfish people stand out!

Greed and pride reign supreme among some people in society. The politician who took bribe money to benefit a special interest. A CEO caught in an ethics violation who still uses a "golden parachute" to exit with millions. Sadly, that behavior grabs the headlines on the evening news and Internet gossip sites (not that we read those, of course!). This "shock value" captures our attention. Deep down, we know it's wrong. Greed and pride, while glamorous to some, do not endure in the minds of those who live for love. The people who exercise temperance and humility find peace and positivity. These are qualities that can't be bought or sold. Likewise, if your mind is clouded with pride and jealousy, it's impossible to receive and give love.

The obstacles to love are negative emotions and thoughts. This means that emotional intelligence is crucial to living a life of love. In his book, *Social Intelligence: The New Science of Human Relationships*, Daniel Goleman quotes Harvard psychology professor Jerome Kagan in talking about how goodness outweighs meanness:

Harvard's Jerome Kagan proposes this mental exercise to make a simple point about human nature: the sum total of goodness vastly outweighs that of meanness. "Although humans inherit a biological bias that permits them to feel anger, jealousy, selfishness and envy, and to be rude, aggressive or violent," Kagan notes, "they inherit an even stronger biological bias for kindness, compassion, cooperation, love and nurture—especially toward those in need." This inbuilt ethical sense, he adds, "is a biological feature of our species." [4]

By choosing to love those around us, we make the world a better place. We become the living embodiment of The Golden Rule.

Value within the Value

Love is also about forgiveness. Have your tissues handy, because this next story is as bold as love can be.

A Story to Tell

On a tragic night in Charleston, South Carolina, in 2015, the lives of Chris Singleton and many other families were turned upside down. During a prayer service at the African Methodist church on Calhoun Street, a terribly disturbed young man walked in and murdered nine people. One of those people, Shardona, was the mother of Charleston Southern baseball player Chris Singleton. It was a time to question, "Why?" and to wonder how something so awful and sad could happen to such wonderful people. In times of tragedy, it's easy for us to think communities will be completely torn apart. Yet, led by the remarkable resolve, maturity, and love in the heart of Chris Singleton, his inspiring act of forgiveness helped a city lead with its heart and display a powerful message of love for all.

The night after the horrific tragedy, Singleton walked up to the microphone at a community gathering of baseball players and residents and said, "Love is always stronger than hate. So, if we just love the way my mom would, then the hate won't be anywhere close to what love is."[5]

"We already forgive him for what he's done. There's nothing but love from our side of the family." [6]

Chris Singleton showed everyone an inspiring example of forgiveness. His bold willingness to love helped heal a community and nation. Chris Singleton is a man whose values should be placed on a pedestal and observed and modeled for all time. That he could think of love during such a time of tragedy gives all of us hope.

The Value of Love

You've undoubtedly read the words from the epigraph for this chapter. They are often read at weddings and have frequently been used in movies. At a Christian wedding, you know it's coming, just like Owen Wilson's character in *Wedding Crashers*. Part of the reason why is because Saint Paul's definition of love is the best most of us have heard. While this comes from the New Testament of the Bible, it's religion-agnostic in its meaning. It's crystal clear about what love is and should be, and how the self-giving nature of love is so pure.

Love is the most important of all values because it is the most fulfilling and lasting. Giving love breathes life into us and those we touch. Whether it's love of our family, romantic love for a partner or spouse, or affectionate love that we show our neighbors or friends, our heart desires to love and be loved. If you are so lucky, perhaps you have or someday will fall in love. Know that this experience alone will not last forever. It is the friendship forged during this experience that will endure and continue to enhance that powerful feeling of falling in love.

" *But let there be spaces in your togetherness and let the winds of the heavens dance between you. Love one another but make not a bond of love: let it rather be a moving sea between the shores of your souls."—Khalil Gibran*

All of us are given the tremendous blessing to love and to be loved. Recognize that these are two different things. The act of loving someone else is self-giving. It is not just a thought—it is an action we take purely with the selfless, altruistic intention of providing benefit for someone else. Accepting love from someone requires that we take into thought the act of being loved. Then, we willingly allow ourselves to be loved. We choose to let the kindness, beauty, and goodness of that indescribable emotion wash over ourselves. Always remain open to love.

Results of Love

If you left the world tomorrow, looking back on your life, who would you remember most? Would it be the people who loved you and helped you become the woman or man you are today? These people who love us leave a legacy—an imprint on our souls. Their love influences the way we think and how we act. They inspire us to want to do the same for others—to make our legacy one of love and genuine care for everyone we meet. We observe that all forms of love are not impulsive reactions. They require thought and concern for others. They're communicated via words and actions that inspire and radiate warmth. Hopefully, you can aspire to be so beautiful. The gifts of gratitude and love will be yours in return.

As you've seen, love manifests itself through passion, affection, and desire for another person. Love can come through the desire to improve ourselves, to better the lives of our family and friends. Our desire to help ourselves and others is embracing a life of love. Love is not self-seeking—love is a gesture from our heart directly intended to please someone else. The age-old saying, "It is better to give than to receive," reinforces this notion and inspires us to serve others with a loving heart.

Serving sometimes means making the ultimate sacrifice: laying down one's life for a friend. Both courage and altruism are acts of love, because there is no selfishness or fear in love.

May love permeate your thoughts, words, and actions. May it give life to your relationships, helping you to build powerful, lasting bonds with your family members, friends, students, and employees. May you love and give that gift to all. We may never know the meaning of life on this earth, but we arrive at peace when we realize the power of love. Loving with all our heart, and receiving love in return, is the most beautiful blessing in life.

Game Plan

1. Write some love letters. That's right, nothin' wrong with being old-fashioned! Deliver a hand-written note to your mom, dad, partner, spouse, child, and close friends. Write from the heart. Let them know how you feel about them. Then, follow up your words with actions. Do three things each week to show devoted, genuine interest to the people you love. This could be picking up groceries, taking on more chores at home or simply giving your Dad a hug to let him know you love him. Take the first step.

2. Chances are, you've done something wrong—at some point— to someone close to you. Maybe you never apologized for your actions. Seek forgiveness, my friend. There's a remarkable power in seeking forgiveness from others. Forgiveness is an act of love, integrity and humility. Forgiveness will repair a relationship that needs mending, opening the way for love.

3. Don't forget—love yourself. Love who you are. To truly love another person, you must be willing to accept who you are, faults and all.

Notes

[1] "Love," *Merriam-Webster*, https://www.merriam-webster.com/dictionary/love (accessed May 30, 2017).

[2] C. S. Lewis, *The Four Loves* (New York: Harcourt Brace, 1960), 1st

[3] H. G. Liddell and Robert Scott, *An Intermediate Greek-English Lexicon: Founded upon the Seventh Edition of Liddell and Scott's Greek-English Lexicon* (Benediction Classics), 4. Note: C. S. Lewis did not actually use the word *agape*. It was later used by others.

[4] Daniel Goleman, *Social Intelligence: The New Science of Human Relationships* (New York: Bantam Dell, 2006), 62.

[5] Watch: Chris Singleton, "Message of love from Charleston victim's son," ESPN, http://www.espn.com/video/clip?id=13380619 (accessed May 30, 2017).

[6] Watch: Chris Singleton, "Love Is Stronger," (Full Feature HD), https://www.youtube.com/watch?v=5MMsVz7IOwQ&t=745s (accessed May 30, 2017).

III
Character

CHAPTER 9

Integrity

"Integrity is choosing courage over comfort; choosing what is right over what is fun, fast, or easy; and choosing to practice our values rather than simply professing them." [1]

— Brené Brown

DEFINITION:

Firm adherence to a code of especially moral or artistic values: incorruptibility [2]

During the 2011 NFL season, there was a lot of clamoring for the New York Giants to fire their head coach, Tom Coughlin. The Giants were 7–7 and on the verge of missing the playoffs. Despite leading the team to a Super Bowl victory four years earlier, the pressure-cooker was getting warm. In New York, the fans or the media are bound to run you out sooner or later. (In many instances, sooner is more like it!)

But Coughlin was prepared to defy the odds. A veteran coach, he had "been there, done that," and this was just another moment of adversity. Still, some were beginning to wonder if Coughlin's act was wearing thin. His coaching style was strict, with a focus on discipline and character. Coughlin was not the typical "player's coach." He was more of a father-figure. He aimed to get the most out of the men he coached, teaching morals and principles, while imparting values-based wisdom on rookies and veterans alike.

As the Giants hit the home stretch, they peeled off two consecutive wins against their biggest rivals—the New York Jets and the Dallas Cowboys. Just like that, the Giants were back in the playoffs. And the rest, as they say, is history. Like he did four years earlier, Coach Coughlin led the Giants through the playoffs, winning three consecutive games en route to a rematch against the New England Patriots in the Super Bowl.

In the big game, Coughlin devised another winning strategy. The Giants defense stymied the high-powered Patriots' offense. New York's offense dominated the time of possession. The Giants were Super Bowl champs for the second time in four years. It was a stunning turnaround, with both the season—and Coughlin's job—on the line. The veteran coach rose to the occasion, and in the process likely assured himself a spot, one day, in the Pro Football Hall of Fame.

How did he do it?

I leave that to four-time All-Pro offensive lineman Chris Snee to explain. He played his entire career for Coach Coughlin and understood his values-based approach to leadership better than anyone: "All he wanted was for us to have complete trust in each other as men and as teammates. He preached integrity and accountability. He demanded it. And if he hadn't—and if we as players didn't respect him enough to deliver on those demands—we wouldn't have had what it took to win two Super Bowls. That all started with him." [3]

The Core of Integrity

66 *Reputation is what others think of you. Character is what you know yourself to be."* — *Coach John Wooden*

While we're talking about integrity, it's equally as important to think of the word that defines the way we view ourselves: character. Character is defined as "one of the attributes or features that make up and distinguish an individual." [4] You're the only one who knows what you do when no one is looking. You know how you use your time and what your thoughts focus around. Character means being the absolute best that you can be, regardless of the "score," or whether anyone is paying attention. Character is what you owe to yourself: your dignity, honesty, integrity, effort, and self-respect.

Ask yourself, "How can I keep building and living a life that is truer to my values and principles?" You and I exhibit strong character when we are true to ourselves. This means less living purely for what "feels good," and more living the life you're called to live, even if you don't yet have the script for what it looks like.

The point is—we're not going to have life figured out in our first twenty or twenty-five years. Even those who appear to have it down are searching for answers just like you and me. The picture gets clearer with time. A person of character has the self-awareness to anticipate these revelations and changes, then pounce on them. That person evolves by using this new information to add on to the masterpiece that God created: themselves.

“I care not what others think of what I do, but I care very much about what I think of what I do! That is character!”— Theodore Roosevelt

We control our thoughts, and they are what can make us great. Living with integrity means living with deep concern for our thoughts and actions. This requires mindfulness for how we influence people and the environment around us. If we are true to ourselves and honest with others, that trust will form the backbone of our relationships and endear us to everyone we meet.

Our actions as women and men of integrity shouldn't be reflective of the reaction—positive or negative—we get. We should act upon the belief that what we're doing is right and noble. Being recognized does matter to all of us, at least to some degree. We're deluding ourselves if we say otherwise. But that's not the reason why we act.

If tomorrow came and no one recognized you or congratulated you for the good work that you do, would you suddenly stop living a life of integrity? Would you think that your positive actions no longer matter? People of integrity do what they do because their character is ingrained in them—their actions are preceded by their code of honor. Integrity is the genuine article.

Integrity is the representation and embodiment of who and what we really are. It's the words we use and how we back them up. Living this value requires implicit faith in ourselves, and that we hold true to our morals and values. As the age-old saying goes, "Don't talk the talk if you can't walk the walk."

Sadly, many in society have lost the desire to hold themselves to a higher standard. We can change that by setting the bar high, defining success, and aiming for the stars. We can look up to famous figures in history like Coach John Wooden, civil rights activist Rosa Parks, and President Theodore Roosevelt. We can turn to present-day examples of integrity like Oprah Winfrey. We may even be best suited to look at people closest to us like our parents, siblings, or friends.

But ultimately, we need to hold ourselves accountable. Step out boldly and start living so that you can become the next role model that friends, peers and others look up to. I encourage you to speak confidently when you have an attitude of expectancy and belief in your ability to back up your words. There's a tremendous power that is unleashed when you take the time to strategize, commit to your goals and speak them over your life.

You amplify this power when you live those words out in action with consistency. In the most important, worldly relationship of all—your relationship with yourself—both words and actions will define you. Take the time to care with greater passion and energy about how you live. You'll begin to attract the people you want to have in your life. You'll live up to your word and promises and continue on the path toward living a life of integrity.

Obstacles to Living with Integrity

- Concern with "getting ahead" by unsavory means

- Living an inauthentic life

- Doing the wrong thing while knowing it's the wrong thing

People can sniff a fake or an inauthentic peddler a mile away. These are the individuals who cut corners, promote their selfish ambitions over the welfare of others, and live by a code of deceit. The saying, "Nice guys finish last" is a bunch of hogwash. Balderdash! Nice gals and guys finish first in the long run. Cheaters finish last. They may appear to "win" by deceptive means, but they'll never really win in the long run.

If we deliberately do the wrong thing and know in our hearts it isn't right, we end up in pain—stomach turning, tight hamstrings, cold sweat. We've all been there. The awful taste of anxiety and defeat. Far worse than that bitter tasting cough syrup in our eternal five-year-old memories!

What distinguishes a person of integrity from a fraud? The person of integrity is deeply concerned with their own perception of their character. They live out the mantra of "Be yourself" in all they do. Those two words stand the test of time for a reason. They're probably the best words of advice you will ever receive. *Be yourself* means that you're an honest, trustworthy person who lives by a code of morals and values. *Be yourself* is fundamental to living a life of integrity.

"Are you going to show integrity only when someone is watching you—or are you going to show it all the time?"— Mike Krzyzewski, Duke University Men's Basketball Head Coach

Think about it—if you sign up to help at your local animal shelter and say you're going to be there at precisely 9:00 on Saturday morning, then make sure you're there at precisely 9:00! Don't let those puppies down! Your duty to your obligations and your fulfillment of them becomes your character.

Authentic people are high-character individuals who don't just "talk the talk," they also "walk the walk." This means, they back up their positive, empowering words with actions that benefit themselves and others. Authenticity is about presence and living in the moment with conviction and confidence. The authentic person puts the people around them at ease. There's never any doubt or questioning the integrity of an authentic individual. Their behavior, in terms of ethics and morals, is as predictable as snow during wintertime in Minnesota. You know what you're going to get.

In our fast-paced professional and personal lives, we don't have time for liars who attempt to mislead or harm us. We want to know that we're dealing with authentic people who will never steer us wrong. In fact, we want someone who will look out for our welfare through their loyalty and friendship. We don't want any surprises from people that we trust. Avoid those who attempt to lead you astray. Work with someone who is authentic and transparent that "shows their cards" in all dealings.

Value within the Value

> *Achievement of your happiness is the only moral purpose of your life, and that happiness, not pain or mindless self-indulgence, is the proof of your moral integrity, since it is the proof and the result of your loyalty to the achievement of your values."*

> — *Ayn Rand*

If values are the GPS that helps us navigate living, then integrity is the human element that ensures we aren't on auto-pilot. Integrity is the glue that holds our thoughts and actions together and forms the fundamental backbone of our character. Integrity is a trait that is most easily observed in human transactions. Maybe not right away, but over time, we can tell when we're dealing with someone who will stand by us through tough times.

A few years ago, I was laid off from my job. It was a stunning blow. I learned that some people, who I thought were my friends, didn't have my back when I needed it most. My manager did. He was a man who cared about my personal and professional success. We met on my last day, and he said these words I'll never forget: "I told you I was invested in your development as a person. Nothing about what has happened now has changed that. Let me know how I can help you, and we'll get to work."

Derrick became a friend and someone who offered support during a challenging time. He regularly met with me to provide mentorship and offer career guidance. Talk about sticking with a man when his chips are down! Derrick stood by his words. He proved that integrity is doing what you say you're going to do. He was willing to demonstrate through actions that he would continue to help me. He didn't care what others thought. He did what he believed was right because he's a man of character and integrity. Every company would be fortunate to have someone like him.

Who is that person for you? Is it someone you see or speak with on a regular basis? Or do you spot this quality in others? Observe it and model your approach after it. Try to give to others the integrity you desire to see in return. This bold value becomes ingrained in you the more you live by it and repeat its time-tested qualities.

Results of Integrity

> *We might think that, provided you did the right thing, it did not matter how or why you did it—whether you did it willingly or unwillingly, sulkily or cheerfully, through fear of public opinion or for its own sake. But the truth is that right actions done for the wrong reason do not help to build the internal quality or character called a 'virtue', and it is this quality or character that really matters."* [5]—C. S. Lewis, *Mere Christianity*

There comes a point where evolution is essential, but unnecessary change is detrimental. We can go through life and keep changing and molding ourselves into something we're not. Most of us want to evolve and continue learning more about ourselves. We have an innate desire to find peace of mind and to reach a feeling of fulfillment in our lives.

No matter how far we stray, we always have our values and morals to ground us. Integrity is not something we can take for granted. Like all values, it's something we must aspire to maintain and build every day. Look inward and, through introspective thought and constructive action, build yourself up and refine your skills. You have control over your destiny. You can choose to live with integrity, no matter your circumstances.

My parents and brothers are the ones who have taught me about integrity. I count my blessings each day that I have the birth family I do. My family taught me to value myself, by instilling in me the belief that I could do big things. My mom and dad have always lived by a code of morals and ethics. Like everyone, they made mistakes—and still do! *(Uh-oh, I hope they're not reading this!)* But they made it very clear what the difference between right and wrong was.

My brothers and I knew there were repercussions for behaving the wrong way. We knew what it meant to make the right decisions. Honesty was valued. Love was always shared. My parents continue to care for their children tremendously. It is this love and interest in who we are as people that set the tone for the rest of our relationship as parents and children. These two towers of integrity have provided me with a life as good as any I ever could have imagined.

Who are the people of integrity in your life? Who are the beacons of honesty, trust, and character that you can turn to, through thick and thin, who will always have your back and serve you well? Hold those people close to your heart and never let them go. Then, return the favor: show them the same integrity that they show you. Integrity is unmistakable when you see it. It's as vivid as the sunset over the Pacific Ocean. As authentic as walking into a big-league park for your first Major League Baseball game. As real as someone standing up for you, no matter the circumstance. As true as being yourself.

Game Plan

1. Who is your role model? Do you have one? Find a person you can observe who lives a life of integrity. Someone who adheres to a code of morals and values. You may not need to look very far. It could be someone you know very well (family or friend). Emulate this person. Observe their

behavior. Start to incorporate their words and actions into your repertoire.

2. Is there something—or someone—you can stand up for right now? It could a cause you believe in. Maybe it's someone you know who you feel has been wronged. Perhaps a co-worker or classmate that is a victim of discrimination. Speaking up and standing up for causes or people you believe in takes integrity and character. Don't be afraid to take a stand. People will notice and respect you for it.

3. Think about the things that matter most to you. Family. Faith. Job. Helping others. Whatever those things are, hold them dear. Always stay true to who you are and what matters most to you. Your feelings toward politics and music may change, but you should always stay true to the values that define you. That's integrity.

Notes

[1] Brené Brown, *Rising Strong: How the Ability to Reset Transforms the Way We Live, Love, Parent, and Lead* (New York: Random House, 2015), 123.

[2] "Integrity," *Merriam-Webster*,

https://www.merriam-webster.com/dictionary/integrity (accessed May 30, 2017).

[3] Chris Snee, quoted in Steve Weatherford, "More Than a Coach," *The Players' Tribune*, January 8, 2016, https://www.theplayerstribune.com/giants-tom-coughlin-tribute-coach/ (accessed May 30, 2017).

[4] "Character," Merriam-Webster,

https://www.merriam-webster.com/dictionary/character (accessed May 30, 2017).

[5] C. S. Lewis, "The Cardinal Virtues," Book 3, ch. 2 of *Mere Christianity* (C.S. Lewis Pte. Ltd., 1952)

CHAPTER 10

Honesty

"Honesty is the first chapter in the book of wisdom."

—Thomas Jefferson

DEFINITION:

(a) Fairness and straightforwardness of conduct (b) adherence to the facts: sincerity [1]

Zero.

In eleventh grade, I was a student in the chemistry class of a teacher who valued honesty above anything. Yes, even more than Bunsen burners and the Periodic table. He was an old-school stickler who prided himself on keeping students in line. More than all the atoms, protons, and elements I could handle, boy was I going to receive a lesson in the value of telling the truth.

When you're in high school, you think you can get away with virtually anything. At least *I* did. There's no one, other than your parents, to tell you that your smart-aleck ways won't fly in the eyes of a 50-year old man. Most of us get wiser with age, as we acquire wisdom and knowledge from thousands of human interactions that improve our truth filter. This filter enables the truth to come marching through and the lies to be stopped dead in their tracks. But during junior year, to my huge disadvantage, I had yet to learn this valuable information.

It was winter, and basketball season was in full swing. My focus was on the game, not on improving my chemistry grades. Earlier on in high school, I had gotten away with cutting a class the day of an exam to give myself more time to study. I thought I'd try this again, without telling my parents.

Didn't it seem like we could always get away with anything at the age of sixteen?

So, I cut. I ended up coming to school halfway through the day so I could practice with the basketball team, but I avoided class. My teacher called me on it. Well, not me, actually. He called my mom directly, at work. While I don't know exactly what was said on that call, I do know what my mom said to me later that evening:

"What is wrong with you?!"

Trust me, it sounded a lot louder in person.

The next day, I walked into class ready to take the exam. The teacher told me to see him after class. When the bell mercilessly sounded to end 3rd period, he put me in my place. He notified me that there would be no make-up exam. I not only failed, I was given a zero on the test. Zero as in 0, zilch, nada, nothing, squadoosh. I'm still not sure what that equals on the pH scale.

Averaging in a zero to other test scores and homework was like plopping down the Tasmanian Devil at a bridal shower. Lots of screaming and crying and enormous work to clean up the mess. My grade suffered mightily that quarter. So did my reputation in the eyes of that teacher. Of course, a lesson came from this mess: Tell the truth.

What I was told during the stern talking-to was, had I simply been honest and told him that I wasn't prepared, I would still have received a failing grade but it wouldn't have been a zero. It would have been a 60. Maybe this teacher simply didn't want to feel outfoxed by a 16-year-old, though it was undeniable he was trying to prove a point that went well beyond a few compounds and mixtures.

Honesty would prevail in his classroom. It was highly advised that I practice it in my academic and athletic pursuits, as well as my relationships. What I thought was simply an innocent lie, at the time, deeply offended his sensibilities and terribly disappointed my mom. She raised me to be honest and virtuous—not to deceive and take the easy way out.

While I was angry and upset over the zero, I also realized that fighting fire with fire would never work. I sucked it up, apologized, and set out to take my schoolwork—and truth-telling—more seriously. My grades improved, the teacher's respect for me grew, and I received an age-old lesson in honesty that has proven invaluable during my life's journey: Honesty is the best policy.

The Core of Honesty

Honesty always seeks the truth, tells the truth, and lives on through actions in a forthright manner. Of all the values, honesty is perhaps the most important and fundamental to human affairs. Honesty begets trust. Without trust, in any type of relationship, we have no foundation or structure. Trust is vital for love, acquiring knowledge, and developing the fulfillment of our best intentions—our true desires.

When you're honest, people will entrust things to you and you'll trust yourself to deliver on what you say and promise. You'll grow in self-respect, and the people around you will respect you. Honesty has, in some ways, unfortunately, become an even more desired characteristic in today's world simply due to the amount of dishonesty. Just look at the most recent presidential election—or any political race for that matter!

While largely out of your control, you still benefit from being honest simply because many people choose to live in deceit and duplicity. Not only will you be ahead of the game by living honestly, you should choose to do so for the right reasons. Honest people live with a clear mind and conscience—and less worry. There's nothing to fear when you tell the truth. In fact, the world around you opens up with opportunity. Living with honesty and integrity affords you the opportunity to live life on your own terms.

Honesty will take you far in life, and it's the easiest thing you can practice to be happy, successful, and fulfilled. Honesty isn't just about telling the truth. It's about being real with yourself and others about who you are, what you want, and what you need to live your most authentic life. Honesty promotes openness, empowers us, and enables us to develop consistency in how we present the facts. Honesty sharpens our perception and allows us to observe everything around us with clarity. Think about it—how do you feel inside when you know you're being lied to, or worse yet, when you're lying to someone else? It makes my stomach turn!

In an honesty experiment conducted by two University of Notre Dame professors, results showed that telling the truth is good for our health:

Recent evidence indicates that Americans average about 11 lies per week. We wanted to find out if living more honestly can actually cause better health. We found that the participants could purposefully and dramatically reduce their everyday lies, and that in turn was associated with significantly improved health.[2]

Respectable, admired behavior is always carried out with honesty. Telling the truth and backing it up with actions shows respect for what's right and esteem for ethical and moral integrity. Honesty is one of the key components to character and one of the most admired traits of any successful, responsible person. Success and happiness is not quantified in terms of dollars, sales, or number of Facebook followers. Particularly not the latter! Peace of mind comes from self-awareness, honesty, kindness, and living a virtuous life. It's about how we treat ourselves and others, and how we use our talents to improve the lives of others.

An emotionally intelligent person is a person of impeccable integrity and honesty, someone who can perceive and recognize the quality of honesty in another. Business transactions and everyday human relations must be carried out with a code of trust and honesty, or everything will break down.

Obstacles to Living with Honesty

- Lying to others

- Lying to ourselves

- Unwillingness to seek the truth

The opposite of honesty is deception—or lying. Lying is equally bad whether you are deceiving others or yourself. When you lie, you delude yourself into believing what you're saying. You start digging a hypothetical ditch, even if with an infant-sized spoon, that will keep getting bigger over time. You confuse yourself and others, lose credibility, and put yourself in harm's way.

The worst type of lying we practice is when we lie to ourselves. We start messing around with our concept of morality, right and wrong, as well as our dreams and desires. The times I lied, to do something that I knew was wrong, I could *feel* it. My inner core rebelled against what I was doing because it contradicted who I really am.

When I look back on it, every time I lied (that I can recall), I was trying to excuse my shortcomings or to compensate for something. I was often pursuing a sinful desire that would only, at best, produce temporary pleasure. Lies I told were due to laziness or a lack of positive intention. Other times, I was convincing myself I wasn't good enough or able to do something my heart was really set on. Lying or presuming I knew something I didn't really know was the easy path. This discouraging thought manifested itself in ways I couldn't perceive at the time. It set me back by delaying the pursuit of my dreams. It took away my ability to take chances that my heart was willing to take but my mind was blocking me from taking.

Lying to ourselves is a slow, painful road to delusion. Lying distorts the facts that we use to analyze information and make decisions. I believe in morality. I believe for those of us born of sane mind, we know right from wrong. We aren't meant to live in deceit by telling lies and confusing ourselves.

Despite its temptation, ease of use, and false promises, lying gets us nowhere in the end. We stay right in our own tracks or much worse, go backwards. It's a temporary illusion, a retreat from the truth and reality. When we lie to others, we're showing them a lack of respect. Ask yourself this: wouldn't you always want your friend, co-worker, classmate, or partner to tell you the truth? Truth is essential because we cannot function at a high-level if we're living in or telling lies. It's utterly ridiculous. Honesty, truth-telling, and truth-seeking are paramount in life. No one is willing to tolerate a dishonest broker.

And yet, just take a look at folks who end up in the news! People in trouble for corruption-related offenses, thieves who swindle people out of money and end up in prison. You likely have friends who have been badly hurt in romantic relationships by people who acted selfishly and lied. Any actions or words said in a fleeting moment can lead to a lifetime of pain and permanent damage to a relationship.

One last obstacle to honesty is the withholding of the truth. This is not quite lying, but a form of deceit that is often deliberate. In most cases like these, we are mindful of what we're doing. We intentionally stay silent, for better or worse. We can look at our relationships and give deep, clear thought to determine if we've sown seeds of deception—even if we've lied about petty things. When we're honest with ourselves, we find when we tell the truth the first time, we're better off.

3 Questions on Honesty to Ask Yourself:

1. Are you letting people know your true self?

2. If not, what are you afraid of?

3. What is the cost to you for telling a lie?

Value within the Value

Step one in personal development is honesty. No doubt about it— you have to be honest with yourself before you can ever be honest with someone else. You have to live the truth that you think and speak over your life. I've always carried myself with a candidness (and I'd like to believe genuineness) that demonstrates a reflection of my thoughts. At times, I've been candid to a fault. But overall, I live with zero regrets. I believe candidness, openness, and honesty have benefited me more in relationships than any other qualities.

Honesty endears us to people of influence, friends and loved ones. Honesty is never contrived or inauthentic—it's always pure and delivered in real time. It's better to lay your cards on the table and be forthcoming and transparent about your aspirations and intents. Leave the deception and lies to intelligence agents in a Jason Bourne movie—in the land of fiction, where they belong.

There's no coincidence that perhaps the most respected American in history, President Abraham Lincoln, is often referred to as Honest Abe. Lincoln was shrewd, direct, and honest in his dealings. He was fair and just, traits he learned while working as a store clerk when he was young. A defining first-hand account of Lincoln comes from Leonard Swett, a close friend of the former president: "He believed in the great laws of truth, the right discharge of duty, his accountability to God, the ultimate triumph of the right, and the overthrow of wrong."[3]

And why not pass along Lincoln's own words on the topic: *"Resolve to be honest at all events; and if, in your own judgment, you cannot be an honest lawyer, resolve to be honest without being a lawyer. Choose some other occupation."*

Do you want to be one of the most respected, highly thought of people in your social circle? Follow the example of the man thought of by many as the greatest president who ever lived. Honesty will define who you are before you even allow others to know more about you. Honesty cuts through red tape, distraction, frustration, and indecision. Honesty gets you where you want to go faster because you live how you really feel. You may not always know what you want in your future—whether that's one month, six months, or two years from now—but your intuition will give you a feel for what is in harmony with your heart.

Results of Honesty

Honesty gives real meaning to words and actions. It's a past, present, and future tense way for us to be at peace with our beliefs and actions. Virtual Reality may bring us away from the present moment on a fun ride of temporary pleasure. Honesty centers us. Dealing with the facts at hand is an everyday necessity. It's always better to deal in the truth, both in thought and action.

Of all relationships in life, few are more underappreciated than the relationship we have with ourselves. A lot of discussions and literature around personal development centers on building relationships and cultivating emotional intelligence, so we can share those gifts with others. To do those things, we first need to share those gifts with ourselves. The way we emotionalize and nurture our thoughts leads us toward living a productive and fulfilling life.

Honest intentions in speech and action gain the attention and respect of others. The company we keep and surround ourselves with helps to define our outlook on life, lifting us to places we couldn't have arrived at entirely by our own efforts. Start today, first, by being as honest as you can with yourself.

Know this, friend: some people will have a problem with you when you tell the truth. They might prefer to be protected by a lie or a cover for their own inappropriate behavior. From the President of the United States to our next-door neighbor, we've seen people of power and influence lie to conceal the truth. In the end, it doesn't get them very far. It's self-defeating and damaging to their reputation. Telling the truth isn't easy. The truth is cold and hard, and many people can't handle it. But it's always the best way to go.

We're emotional creatures. In the heat of the moment, we may take things the wrong way and overreact. We're also protective of ourselves. We don't want to be made fun of. We sometimes seek comfort and refuge in lies, ironically, because they're a distortion of reality. Lies help us procrastinate and avoid our present moment. Know that lies only take you away from who you are and where you want to be. Better to play things straight-up and tell the truth. You'll ace the exam, and pass with flying colors.

Game Plan

1. Make a commitment to yourself: write a contract that you will tell the truth. There may be times that this hurts you—in the short-term. There will be friends or co-workers who ask you to "cover for them" and tell a white lie on their behalf. What may seem innocuous at the time is really a long-term trap. Tell the truth. Authentic people deal in truth and facts. We all want to be trusted, and being honest is the way to achieve trust.

2. Ask your friends and loved ones to hold you accountable to telling the truth. For added incentive, consider some small penalties for telling a lie. Think of it like an honesty "swear jar." Each time you lie, you pay $5. Too harsh? Well, hurting yourself and others with a lie is much more damaging.

Notes

[1] "Honesty," *Merriam-Webster*,

https://www.merriam-webster.com/dictionary/honesty (accessed May 23, 2017).

[2] Press Release, "Lying Less Linked to Better Health, New Research Finds," American Psychological Association, August 4, 2012, http://www.apa.org/news/press/releases/2012/08/lying-less.aspx (accessed May 23, 2017).

[3] Gordon Leidner, *A Commitment to Honor: A Unique Portrait of Abraham Lincoln in His Own Words* (Nashville, TN: Thomas Nelson, 2000) Chapter 3, Faith

CHAPTER 11

Respect

"If you want to be respected by others, the great thing is to respect yourself. Only by that, only by self-respect will you compel others to respect you."

— *Fyodor Dostoyevsky*

<u>DEFINITION:</u>

High or special regard: esteem.[1]

The greatest admiration and respect that I have is for those who risk their lives to protect our freedoms. For four years, I had the honor of working with servicemen and women in the United States Army and Air Force. My business consulting job allowed me to travel across the United States, seeing first-hand the great work they do. I observed the profound respect they have for their duty and service to their country.

On one of my trips, I went to the island of Oahu, in Hawaii. I was on assignment at Joint Base Pearl Harbor-Hickam in Honolulu, working with staff from the Pacific Air Force major command.

A great tradition of the U.S. military is "reveille and retreat,"[2] two ceremonies that signal the start and end of each day on military bases and installations. Music is played over all loudspeakers on the base, and service members must stop what they're doing, stand, and face the base headquarters and offer a salute. If you've never witnessed this—or even been on a military installation—I hope you one day will have the opportunity. It is a sight and moment that is unlike any other patriotic gesture I've ever experienced.

I traveled with my Air Force boss, a lieutenant colonel, someone I considered a mentor. On a base like Pearl Harbor-Hickam, it was a big deal to see a high-ranking officer. In Washington, D.C., where we worked, it was more commonplace to see colonels and even, generals. I recognized this right away. I could see the signs of respect offered by enlisted men and women, as well as other officers, who saluted my boss. Even I was the beneficiary of some very fine treatment, simply by association.

As we prepared to leave the base for the day, the clock struck 5:00 p.m. (or 1700 hours in military time). I looked at my boss and watched with appreciation. I saw the respect he showed the flag and his country. As "Taps" played over the loudspeakers, the chills ran down my spine. Everything seemed frozen in time in that one moment. No one moved. I gazed out at Pearl Harbor—site of the Japanese bombing that brought the United States into World War II. I thought of the men and women who lost their lives on that "date that will live in infamy." I thought of those in our military, around the world, who serve their country each day. I thought of how much this country means to so many people. Truly, America is a land of opportunity that affords its people an abundant life.

I stood there in silence, thinking on all these things, showing my respect, as well. For those soldiers, this was the end of their day. For

me, it was a powerful moment that showed the meaning of respect—
a powerful value to behold.

The Core of Respect

"	*There is no respect for others without humility in one's self."* —
Henri Frederic Amiel

Respect, as they say, is a two-way street. This is when we're
specifically referring to respect for one another. But there are two
distinct types of respect: respect for our peers and respect for
ourselves. As I show in Chapter 9, living with integrity means
treating individuals who are worthy of respect, with respect. Of most
importance, however, is to treat yourself with respect. Think about
it, my friend: you can't truly respect someone else unless you respect
yourself first.

Self-respect is synonymous with growth. It means greater respect
for your self-worth and appearance. Self-respect guides us to be kind
to ourselves and to appreciate life's most valuable commodity: time.
Self-respect is the contract you sign with yourself. When you sign a
contract, you agree to a particular set of terms. This becomes your
obligation. Self-respect is thus an obligation—a promise—that you
will do what you say you're going to do. This means that you write,
think, and speak positive affirmations over your life. It asks you to
view yourself in a confident, considerate manner. Anything less than
living up to the values and high standards that you set is a form of
disrespect to yourself.

As we progress through our lives, we begin to make sense of our
personal relationships and professional pursuits. We recognize and

appreciate the importance of respect. We witness the way it's doled out and realize that we want a part of it. All of us, even the introverts among us, crave respect and outward recognition. Above anything else, we want to feel acknowledged and appreciated by our peers. A lack of respect can lead to a low feeling of self-worth, which causes envy, fear, and doubt to threaten our thoughts.

The best way to receive respect from others is to treat yourself with greater respect. This is a gift of kindness and self-confidence we all can give. People tend to recognize confidence instinctively. Confidence attracts like-minded people into our lives, whether it's people who want to build the next skyscraper—like the Empire State Building—or those looking to create the next social media company, like Facebook. Respect travels in groups. We tend to carry ourselves with more confidence when we're respected by our peers.

Respect is always genuine. Admiration is a form of respect for someone's craft or the way one carries him or herself. I think of great athletes like Roger Federer and Simone Biles. These are individuals who carry themselves with class, grace and remarkable dedication to their craft. They are two of the greatest athletes in the world, yet they treat everyone—from fans, to stadium employees, to their fiercest competitors—with dignity and grace.

When you think of how respect has shown itself in your life, what comes to mind? What people stand out as models of respect that have helped to shape the way you view this value? I think of my parents, brothers, wife, and my grandmother. These are all people I hold in high esteem, not just because I love them, but because of the way they treat others. The example they've shown has inspired me to treat everyone I meet with respect.

Obstacles to Living with Respect

- Criticism

- Low self-esteem

- Lack of self-awareness

- Mean or bad intention to hurt others

Bad habits can form at a young age and carry on throughout life, if not corrected. It's important to highlight this in the context of a lack of respect toward ourselves. This can arise from a feeling of low self-estccm. Sometimes, we all feel inadequate. In the case of Serena Williams, for much of her youth, she endlessly compared herself to her big sister, Venus. Venus was better, thinner and more graceful. This led to Serena feeling like she wasn't good enough. Despite her incredible talent, she struggled with her sense of self-worth. Fast-forward twenty years, and this all seems hard to imagine.

"Most women athletes are pretty thin. I didn't really know how to deal with it. I had to come to terms — as every teen and young adult does — with loving myself." [3]

Serena Williams is now the greatest women's tennis player to ever live. The teenager with low self-esteem matured into a confident, self-assured woman before the world's eyes. If Serena Williams can struggle with self-respect, the best of us can. But we should never turn a lack of respect for ourselves into disrespect and criticism of others.

When someone chooses to criticize another person, they are usually trying to bring attention to themselves. By hurting someone else, they try to look better by comparison. In reality, all they're doing is disrespecting themselves. Whether done one-on-one or (almost always) in a group setting, criticism comes from the giver's desire to elevate him or herself over someone else.

None of us likes to be criticized. We place a high value on our thoughts and physical appearance. We don't want others to hurt us or pick on us. It's especially hurtful when there's an audience around to deepen the wounds of verbal jabs. In these instances, we're better off taking the high road and treating others with respect. Turn the other cheek in unavoidable situations and walk away.

Respect teaches us to treat everyone with dignity. This includes ourselves! We should treat others the way we want to be treated, while never stooping below that high standard. We're sensitive creatures who care about what other people think. We all want to be respected.

Value within the Value

"Respect yourself enough to walk away from anything that no longer serves you, grows you, or makes you happy." — Anonymous

Sports is the vehicle that has taught me so much about respect. Sports serve as the framework for how I view this value. Of all the lessons sports teach, respect and self-sacrifice are the most important ones. When those two things aren't there, it's much harder to succeed. The same applies to any team goal we pursue.

Whether in a band, classroom setting, working group, or volleyball team looking to spike its opponent, respect makes a huge difference.

Over time, we gradually forget most of the wins and highlight reel plays. Don't get me wrong, winning is incredible—and no one forgets a championship. (Especially Red Sox fans—they had to wait eighty-six years, after all!) But basic core values like respect and trust are forged on the field of competition during good times and bad. We remember the hard work we put in and the signs of respect received along the way. We remember our first piano recital after months of instruction, or the treehouse we constructed with our parents. It's the process—the journey—that we often remember more than the moment of final reward. What matters is that we cared and respected each other and that, together, we created something special.

You'll grow, prosper, and gain the respect of others when you care passionately about the result, not so much who gets the credit. It may sound counter-intuitive, because surely, some will only pay attention to those who win the awards. But in the end, those things fade away like footprints on the seashore. What lasts is the impact you make on the lives of those you touch.

You'll find the respect you think you crave is not as valuable as the silent, more powerful type of respect that comes from your peers. People are always watching what we do, both online and in personal interactions. I've found people won't always congratulate you when you're doing well, but they'll tell you if you've done something wrong! As my boss told me when I was sports director of my college radio station: "I'll point out when you're doing things wrong. But I won't always tell you when you're doing well. You'll know the difference." We all want to be respected. Respect or not, keep going. Move forward with confidence when you know you're doing the right thing!

3 Questions on Respect to Ask Yourself:

1. Who are the people you respect most?

2. What is it about their ideals and how they carry themselves that leaves a positive impression on you?

3. Do you treat yourself with self-respect?

A Story to Tell

I'll bet you have someone special in your life who has helped shape the way you respect and treat others. Think about that person right now. Go on, close your eyes. Take a few moments, and give some thought to how special and unique that person made or makes you feel. For me, that person was my Grandma Mary, a truly beautiful woman of class and grace.

In rich times and in poor, my Grandma took outstanding care of herself and her possessions. She taught me family values and how to take care of myself. Oh yeah, and how to treat her 1985 Toyota Camry like a Rolls Royce. That baby was as clean as a whistle! She was always quick to point out life lessons to me, and instilled in me a spirit of faith and confidence. Most importantly, she taught me what it meant to respect myself and the people around me.

My Grandma was a God-fearing woman of deep faith, who impressed upon her children and grandchildren the value of time. She told us it only took a few minutes each day to invest in building our character, and that being a person of our word meant living by example, so others could see.

From the way she dressed, to the immaculate condition in which she kept her apartment, she always greeted everyone with a smile and a generous helping of respect. She made everyone feel like a million bucks. She listened, showed interest in what someone had to say, and cared for others. She behaved like a lady in the presence of company, whether with perfect strangers or family. Her gifts to me were thoughtful and inspiring—always affectionate and personal.

She had razor sharp wit and incredible New York street-smarts. She "killed 'em with kindness" and lived by a code of morals and ethics that she would never compromise for anyone. She never missed an opportunity to tell me how proud she was of me and all I had accomplished, even when I didn't feel the same way inside. She loved me and made me feel special.

So, I ask again, who is that person for you? Learn from them. If you haven't found them yet, perhaps you can use my Grandma's example as a valuable standard of respect to seek in this world. It will be well worth your time.

Results of Respect

Part of respect is what I would dub "the good kind of pride." The respect offered to a competitor following a game. The courtesy shown to an elderly person. Our respect for family tradition, religious tradition, our parents, or the rules and policies of a school or institution. These are the signs of respect that make the world go 'round. These actions result in creating a loving, bolder world to live in.

Respect and kindness go hand-in-hand. They are so, so simple and yet highly valued, because their net results are so positive. Both of these values lead to character, which is how we define ourselves. They contribute to our outward projection to the world—our reputation. I've found we all want to leave a legacy. Ask yourself: If this were your last week on earth, how would you want to be remembered? What would you want friends and strangers alike to think when they remember your life?

Some of the most dynamic figures in world history like, Martin Luther King Jr., Mahatma Gandhi and Mother Teresa, were people who earned everyone's respect for the way they lived their lives. They provided value for others. They respected themselves and believed their self-worth was great. They also believed the people they fought for had very high self-worth! They fought for equal rights, freedom and respect for the people they represented.

Respect begets a desire for altruism and true love for one another. Respect, at its best, is a pure act of care, kindness, friendship and love. Just remember, it all begins with you. Look inward. Start with self-respect. Then, look outward and make the effort to treat your fellow men and women with respect. You may just carve out your own, magnificent place in history.

Game Plan

1. Start thinking about your self-worth. Jot down the words that come to mind. Make a concerted effort to think more about

your well-being. Enter into a positive state of mind by thinking of things you love. Think of the things that excite you. Then, start re-examining the relationship you have with yourself. Are you too tough on yourself? Are you your biggest critic? Learn to respect yourself for who you are right now. This will form the foundation for self-confidence and how you respect others.

2. Lead from the heart. Treat others the way you would like to be treated. Respect the privacy of others, respect what they have to say, and be slow to correct them. People will notice. When you combine self-respect with respect for others, people will come to appreciate and respect you in return. They'll learn they can't take advantage of you. They'll recognize your emotional intelligence. They'll view you as a caring individual who has his/her priorities in order.

Notes

[1] "Respect," Merriam-Webster, https://www.merriam-webster.com/dictionary/respect (accessed May 31, 2017).

[2] Robert, "Customs and Traditions of the Military," MilitarySpouse, http://militaryspouse.com/spouse-101/customs-and-traditions-of-the-military/ (accessed May 31, 2017).

[3] Sasha Bronner, "Serena Williams: 'I Had To Come To Terms With Loving Myself'" The Huffington Post, http://www.huffingtonpost.com/2015/06/18/serena-williams-body-image_n_7599214.html (accessed March 21, 2017)

CHAPTER 12

Discipline (Self-Control)

"You have power over your mind—not outside events. Realize this, and you will find strength."

— *Marcus Aurelius*

DEFINITION:

Self-control: Restraint exercised over one's own impulses, emotions, or desires [1]

Discipline: Training that corrects, molds, or perfects the mental faculties or moral character. [2]

I arrived on campus in the fall of my freshman year ready to have a good time. I was excited to play college basketball, and eager to enjoy all the extracurricular—er—activities that college offers. Study hall? Ha! More like party and meet girls, hit the bars for some drinks (legal drinking age be damned) and play some ball. Oh yeah, and go to class and learn! The way my mind worked at that juncture, sadly, that was the order. My priorities were off.

College is a shock to everyone's system at first, because for many of us, it's the first time we're free and completely on our own. It's also the first time we're tasked with the complete day-to-day management of our lives without any parental assistance. No mom and dad to keep us in line in case we sleep in and miss class. No one to tell us we probably shouldn't go to that off-campus party ... and drink too much ... the night before a major exam. Discipline is in our hands and at our discretion. And that can be a very scary thing, particularly if we're not mentally and emotionally prepared to face our challenges.

One month into my freshman year, the college athletic department held an athlete's symposium that educated us on NCAA requirements. They also brought in a guest—a former college football player and motivational speaker—who was all fired up and ready to inspire. His goal was to awaken us to the destructive reality of drug and alcohol abuse and excessive partying. I thought, oh boy, here's an older guy ready to tell all of us teenagers and early twenty-somethings how not to make the same mistakes he did. Yawn! But the better part of me kept an open mind and paid attention to the words Mike Green[3] said. They were powerful, moving, and thought-provoking. They forever changed my course in college.

Mike explained what it meant to be a college athlete. He let us know it was a privilege to play a college sport, and that we could throw it all away with a few careless decisions. He relayed his own experiences as a college athlete, explaining how alcohol and drugs nearly destroyed his life. He talked about excuses. He told us that a habit of making excuses commences a gradual, downward spiral toward self-destruction. Then, he stood at the front of the room and rattled off a gigantic list of excuses like he was in a rap battle with Eminem.

He told us the excuses we make in life distract us from what our top priorities and goals are. He used an assortment of holidays and events to list the typical drinking days for college students and adults alike. He provided rare psychological insight into why we make the decisions we do, and how we let our minds deceive us into thinking that what is truly worst for us is best.

By the time Mike finished speaking, the room gave him a standing ovation. It was a funny and uplifting introduction to the arena of becoming a NCAA athlete. It was a wake-up call to the importance of how I conducted myself, drove my college career, and represented the school and basketball team. I realized we need to be shrewd and aware of how we choose to spend our social time. That requires discipline. I think about it often in the context of the man I've become, and how all of us can apply the value of self-control to our lives.

Excuses are worthless. We will soar high if we eliminate excuses from our vocabulary. We can delude ourselves into believing falsehoods, and we can justify any actions in our minds. That's how powerful our imagination is. I encourage you to instill rigor and discipline around a set of core values that align with your purpose. By doing so, you'll live a productive and fulfilling life. You'll also gain the respect of the person who is most responsible for holding you accountable—you.

The Core of Discipline

 Discipline is the bridge between goals and accomplishment."[4] — Jim Rohn

Discipline and self-control are part of our attitude, which means they are always within our control. While our environment certainly contributes to our successes and failures, we cannot control outside events. Living by a code of conduct means that we train our minds to behave a certain way, and that we shun indulgences and desires that are only ephemeral—not lasting in nature.

We have the incredible power to will ourselves to carry out daily tasks, achieve our goals and find happiness. Our self-control is directly impacted by our willpower. Further, self-control is easier to implement into our daily routine when we adhere to a set of core values. Success and happiness are the products of a life lived on principles and values. Discipline is what makes this possible.

Think of discipline as the bonding agent that holds together the take-home art project that often is our lives: disparate pieces somehow working together, despite falling *just short* of a Rembrandt.

A disciplined life is a daily commitment. It's not just a plant we water once a week, like a cactus. When we rise each day, we have to find it in ourselves to discipline our behavior and choices. Daily temptations will confront us all, no matter how virtuously we live. We grow in strength and resolve when we turn down that extra drink, because we know we have to drive home to help our partner with dinner. We become more resilient when we use an hour after dinner to study for the GMAT, rather than watching a rerun of *Real Housewives of Atlanta*. Trust me, it's better not to watch the first time!

Obstacles to Living with Discipline

" *Everybody in the world is seeking happiness—and there is one sure way to find it. That is by controlling your thoughts. Happiness doesn't depend on outward conditions. It depends on inner conditions."* [5] *— Dale Carnegie*

- Lack of control over your actions

- Unwillingness to "do the work" and examine your life for improvement

- Knowing you're doing the wrong thing ... and doing it anyway

- Settling for less

Live life on your terms, with rigor, dedication, and commitment to the greatest extent that you can. Don't make the mistake of settling for anything less than what you deserve. Give thought to the job you work in and how you spend your free time. If you're spending your time on things that don't fulfill you, then maybe this is your time to re-evaluate your circumstances. Don't convince yourself that a job or activity is fine when you know in your heart it's not. When you keep trying to fit the square peg into the round hole, you need to know when to stop. Refresh and reboot your thinking to get back to the disciplined, confident state of mind where you feel unstoppable and indestructible.

The same mindset applies to your personal life and how you choose to let people in. Discipline and self-control enable you to attract the people who are meant to be part of your life's destiny.

These are people who will enrich you and bring you peace, love, and hope. This is why I passionately believe we don't just meet new people by accident or random chance. Our energy, attitude, and thoughts attract people. They are meant to cross our path for a reason.

Living with self-control means being specific, making decisions with deep focus and sticking to them with persistence and determination. What you truly desire should come naturally to you when you live with values and principles. You learn that discipline is a value of repetition. Discipline isn't always sexy or fun, but it's the sure thing. You have to live it all the time to believe in yourself and behave with confidence. When you live without discipline, life doesn't come naturally to you, despite how much energy you waste thinking that it will. You lack control over your actions. This can lead to a lack of confidence. Always strive to operate from a position of confidence each day.

3 Questions on Discipline to Ask Yourself:

1. How do you hold yourself accountable for your actions—good and bad?

2. Do you rely too much on others to hold you accountable?

3. Is there anything in your life that you consider to be out-of-control right now? Think about how it's gotten there and what you're willing to do about it.

Value within the Value

" *We are never going to enjoy stability, we are never going to enjoy spiritual maturity until we learn how to do what's right when it feels wrong, and every time you do what's right by a decision of your will using discipline and self-control to go beyond how you feel, the more painful it is in your flesh, the more you're growing spiritually at that particular moment."—Joyce Meyer*

Having the discipline and willpower to invest greater care in your life may sound trivial to some, but it's everything to those of us who have struggled to find our footing in life. Many of us believe that we will be able to stop on a dime and give up any particular vice or behavior—whenever we feel like it.

Now, ask yourself this question: When has that ever worked for you? Chances are, not very often.

Anything worth achieving and working for will involve sacrifice and discipline. Each time in my life that I've lost weight, I've had to reduce my consumption of carbohydrates, particularly fast food and soda. When I've wanted to improve my intelligence, I've become a voracious reader, inquisitive thinker, and fact-finder. In becoming a high school basketball coach, I sacrificed time I could have spent improving in other areas.

We are who we are because of the decisions we make. By choosing to do one thing, we often choose not to do something else. This requires serious thought, to analyze and be informed on a given direction. It's decisions like these that we'll face time and again in life, never knowing for certain what the outcome will be. We're going to have to make very firm, definite decisions if we want to live a happy, self-controlled life. Our future will become clearer and we'll become more disciplined once we establish this firmness in decision making.

A Story to Tell

" *The ability to subordinate an impulse to a value is the essence of the proactive person." — Stephen R. Covey*

What would you do if you woke up one day and realized your lifelong dreams felt like they were slipping away? That you got on the treadmill of life and kept running, seemingly in the right direction, but once it started speeding up, you struggled to catch-up? You stop to reflect and look back. The present is good, not great. Perhaps it's just lukewarm enough that it makes you comfortable and unwilling to look back at where you've been—and to the future.

Seven years ago, I sat down at my kitchen table with a notebook and pen for a moment of reckoning. I had spent the previous seven years floating around, first in the corporate world, then in graduate school, without much direction. I didn't know what I wanted to do.

Have you been there before?

I had broken up for a second time with my future wife. My social life consisted of hard partying and a serious lack of focus. I didn't have enough discipline to take my job seriously. I was making good money, had a nice apartment and a luxury car. Everything looked great from the outside. But inside, I was deeply unsatisfied. I wasn't living the life that I wanted. I was living someone else's life.

What brought me to that day at my kitchen table wasn't so much one single moment, as much as it was the accumulation of hundreds of moments and literally millions of thought impulses. I wanted to change my ways and live with greater discipline. It was discipline I was lacking, and I knew it. I had to act to find larger meaning and happiness in what I was doing. Only then could I change and follow my heart to where it would lead me.

As I began to open the pages of my notebook and think about what was next, the thoughts that entered my mind were:

I need to start doing what I want. I have to find a way to integrate the things that I love, the dreams I have into my life. Maybe they can be a part of my work day, maybe a part of my social life and perhaps they're a new career away. But I have to start now, and I need to live with self-control and discipline if I'm ever going to make them come true.

It was the first time in my life that the good kind of fear started to settle in my mind. I finally said to myself what I was subconsciously thinking for a while: *you really may be on a bland, meandering path to nowhere. Time to wake up.*

What about you? Do you ever wake up thinking, "Today will be the day! I'm going to learn the purpose and meaning for my life today." Has it ever worked?! Looking back on it, I guess I thought the meaning of my life would just sort of come to me like a wondrous epiphany—BOOM! "Now I get it, I'm meant to _____."

Uh, not so much.

As you've probably realized, it doesn't work that way. Even when outstanding opportunities present themselves, our minds need to be favorable and prepared to accept them. I had to ask myself some tough questions. *What do I want to do? What do I love? What are the most important things in my life?*

One of the activities that came out of this soul-searching was the desire to write a book. I wrote for my school newspaper in high school and college, and writing has always been one of my biggest passions. While I wasn't prepared to drop everything, and become a writer full-time, I knew I needed to discipline myself and start writing more. I needed more enthusiasm and motivation in my life, which in turn would increase consistency in how I approached each day. I made a promise to write and never give up. Some of the words in this book were first written in the days that followed my personal moment of reckoning.

It paid off big-time. I started to see the value of doing more of what I loved, showing up each day with higher energy, verve, and enthusiasm. That translated into a consistent approach at my job. I became a better planner. I kept wanting more of what would propel me into a future—still uncertain—of doing what I loved, while delivering results daily.

What are those passions for you? Have you done this soul-searching yet? Once you do, you might be shocked by the results. But don't be afraid. Have the discipline to go in the direction your heart is leading you.

Results of Discipline

The results of living a life with discipline are a more fulfilling, rewarding life lived on your terms. Discipline gives us a strong willpower to reject the negative and empower the positives. Self-control is, in many ways, self-explanatory. When you live a more disciplined life, you have greater control over your thoughts and actions. You act according to high moral standards, values, and a commitment to success.

Discipline is required for us to be more productive, to love more, and to maximize the gifts and talent we've received in this life. Discipline guards against excuses and prevents us from harming ourselves and those we love. Be willing to do the work and examine your life for improvement. One of the worst mistakes you can make is to continue doing the wrong thing while knowing you're doing the wrong thing. Not only do you have to live with those results, so do your loved ones and friends.

You owe it to yourself to strive to be better. You owe it to yourself to place your priorities, dreams, and goals above the excuses and distractions that threaten to derail you. Life, like basketball, can be a game of limiting negatives. In basketball, the team that turns the ball over to their opponent is bound to lose. In life, when we don't instill discipline in our daily approach, we keep making the same mistakes. The more we take care of ourselves and take ownership over our choices, the greater likelihood we will win at whatever we pursue.

Discipline is not easy. But living a disciplined life should not be a struggle. There's a difference. We'll find ourselves time and again at the proverbial crossroads, forced to make big decisions, all of which require sound judgment and discipline. Choose wisely. Remember to soak it all in as you gaze at what you leave in your wake, while moving forward with what you need. What matters most isn't just what you take with you, it's what you don't take with you. At its essence, that's what discipline means. Decide what you're going to take with you. And decide what you're going to leave behind. Do so with confidence, shaped by the experiences and values that guide your thoughts and actions.

Game Plan:

1. It's always best to count on yourself, because whether it's a workout partner, friend, or co-worker, we never know if that person will always be there. Discipline requires self-reliance at its core. This is why repetition and consistency matter. Live each day with consistent output in the way you treat others, the effort you give and how you stay true to yourself.

2. Mindfulness is presence and awareness in the moment. Mindfulness helps us make sense of our emotions, allowing us to process the way we feel and to clearly interpret what's taking place around us. I encourage you to block out distractions, both external and internal. Be mindful of your surroundings and focus diligently on the moment.

3. Commit to a plan for what you want in your life and what you don't. Cut down on mistakes, excuses and time-wasters. The more you do, the more you'll be able to focus on what matters most. As author Cal Newport says, "what we choose to focus on and what we choose to ignore—plays in defining the quality of our life."[6]

Notes

[1] "Self-control," *Merriam-Webster*, https://www.merriam-webster.com/dictionary/self-control (accessed May 14, 2017).

[2] "Discipline," *Merriam-Webster*, https://www.merriam-webster.com/dictionary/discipline (accessed May 14, 2017).

[3] Mike Green, president and founder of Collegiate Consultants. For more information, visit http://www.mikegreeny.com/aboutus.html.

[4] Jim Rohn quote, http://www.goodreads.com/quotes/28439-discipline-is-the-bridge-between-goals-and-accomplishment (accessed March 10, 2017)

[5] Dale Carnegie, *How to Win Friends and Influence People* (NY: Simon & Schuster, 1981).

[6] Cal Newport, *Deep Work: Rules for Focused Success in a Distracted World, Chapter 3* (NY: Grand Central Publishing, 2016)

IV
Spirit

CHAPTER 13

Competitive Greatness

"If you put your effort and concentration into playing to your potential, to be the best that you can be, I don't care what the scoreboard says at the end of the game, in my book we're gonna be winners!" [1]

— *Norman Dale, Hoosiers*

DEFINITION:

"Perform at your best when your best is required. Your best is required each day." [2]

Joe DiMaggio, the Hall of Famer and New York Yankees great, embodied competitive greatness. Once asked by a reporter why he hustled every play of the game, "Joe D" responded, "Because there might have been somebody in the stands today who'd never seen my play before, and might never see me again. I owe him my best."[3]

For Joe DiMaggio, image was important. From style, to the woman he married (Marilyn Monroe), to how gracefully he ran on a baseball diamond, Joe D always wanted to look good—both on and off the field. Most of all, he wanted to make a lasting impact. He knew the way to do that was to perform at the peak of his abilities every time. That was no small feat, considering the "Yankee Clipper" played a sport that jammed 154 games into a six-month period. And for DiMaggio, that also meant a few games (almost) every year in October.

He is perhaps best known for a record that may stand the test of time: a 56-game consecutive hitting streak which he set in 1941. Such a feat takes resolve, desire, and painstaking focus. DiMaggio's drive for personal and team success was legendary. Despite missing three consecutive seasons—in the prime of his career due to military service in World War II—he returned in 1946 to make the All-Star team. One year later, he won his third MVP award, and the Yankees were once again World Series champions. In fact, DiMaggio won nine World Series titles with the Yankees in thirteen seasons.

(Did I mention I'm a die-hard Yankees fan?!)

Unless you're a professional athlete, your daily routine likely doesn't involve performing in front of 50,000 fans. These days, with the ability to work remotely, you may even work from home. In that case, the only one watching and judging your performance is, well, you. But audience should never matter. What does matter is the way you motivate yourself to achieve your goals, and how you make the most of your God-given talents. Competitive greatness is a mindset anyone can adopt. It's about pride in your performance and focus on the task at hand—like waiting for your pitch and crushing it out of the park, on a towering shot to right-field.

The Core of Competitive Greatness

Competitive greatness sits at the pinnacle of legendary college basketball coach John Wooden's Pyramid of Success.[4] Throughout my journey as a student, basketball coach, business professional, and writer, I've earnestly searched for the answers to how successful people make it to the top—and stay there. I long wondered, why is competitive greatness the top block of Coach Wooden's pyramid? The reason, I have learned, is because first we have to build our foundation in personal development. This is comprised of the building blocks at the base of Coach Wooden's pyramid, and includes values like confidence, industriousness, enthusiasm (fire) and self-control. We need these essential values to perform at the best of our abilities each day.

Competitive greatness is a mindset that is always on, even when we're not officially "in the arena" competing. It never turns off. It's the powerful drive that sustains us and pushes us toward our goals. It's inspired by a desire to achieve and advance in the direction of whatever we set out to accomplish. For you and me, this is the maximum, adrenaline-fueled zenith of self-satisfaction and aspiration that powers us toward reaching our peak potential.

Competitive greatness is a value and an experience. By utilizing this value, we optimize our thinking, which leads us to acquire the skills that we need to be our best. These energetic thoughts enlighten us, stoking the fire of competition that propels us toward our goals. In sport, music, business, and academia, the people we admire most aren't necessarily the most talented; rather, they're the ones who make the most of their talents. People who always give their best are respected and are most likely to succeed.

" You can't always be the strongest or most talented or most gifted person in the room, but you can be the most competitive."[5] — Coach Pat Summitt

As another legendary basketball coach would tell you, the late, great Pat Summitt, we're all born with unique talents. It is a fool's errand to wish we were someone else. Dreaming and desiring the natural abilities of others won't get us very far. We eventually arrive at the realization that we are uniquely created! All of us are given special gifts, specifically crafted for our lives. The talents, physical traits, skills, and learning aptitude we possess are sufficient for our needs.

From there, it's up to us to use these characteristics to our advantage, by melding them with a burning desire to want to perform at our best, without any regret.

Obstacles to Living with Competitive Greatness

- Lethargy

- Apathy

- Willingness to settle (status quo)

- Lack of passion

The obstacles to competitive greatness can either be hurdles that you leap over or roadblocks that deny you future progress. A competitive mindset isn't about living in competition with others. It's not about worrying whether you'll measure up to someone else's definition of success. A competitive mindset empowers you to demand the most of yourself. It's a reminder always to think like a winner—and then act like one.

The willingness to settle, often fueled by a lack of passion, can be devastating to achieving a competitive mindset. Each day, we all face challenges and obstacles that threaten to throw us off-course. These appear in our daily routines or in unexpected ways like a major, time-sensitive project that lands on our desk on a Friday afternoon... right before our weekend trip to the beach. Don't you hate that? Sometimes, it could just be getting out of the house in the morning if we have a toddler kicking, screaming, and crying. I know the feeling!

There's stress that comes from meeting deadlines at work and taking care of responsibilities around the house. We're charged to maintain equanimity in the face of adversity, financial difficulties, and health issues. These factors can amount to an overwhelming burden very quickly, if we're not ready to face them with all we've got. We all go through days where we feel anxious, helpless, or tired. These emotions can cause us to feel less inspired. Competitive greatness takes time and energy to be cultivated. While obstacles like apathy and lack of passion are real impediments, they're more apt to target us if we simply sit still. Inaction is often our worst enemy.

Competitive greatness comes in a variety of forms. It may manifest itself in your extracurricular activities, or it could simply be the call to rise at the beginning of each day. This means providing for your family, working toward your education, showing up to your job, and giving your very best effort. Any effort or attitude that settles for less than your best is simply unacceptable.

Everything we are and everything we can become is earned by the way we compete. And compete we must, if we expect to improve and reach the lofty goals we set for ourselves. Identify the obstacles that stand in your way. Be honest. Once you can identify what holds you back, you're better positioned to give your best effort and performance, regardless of "the score." Practice consistency every day, so you can make every day your masterpiece.

Value within the Value

Someday, if we're fortunate, we will wake up each morning to pursue our life's work, in some shape, form, or fashion. This is attainable when we compete hard and long enough, with persistence, patience, and an attitude of expectancy. Maybe you're just beginning to think of what a rewarding life this could be—of what doing the work you were placed on this earth to do might look like. Maybe you're on the path now. Better yet, perhaps you've already arrived there.

Along the way, you will already have established your mission and purpose. Your hours, days, and years of learned experiences will be worth their weight in gold as you develop your acumen and steel your resolve to compete harder and with greater dedication each day. When you get there, the feeling of self-fulfillment and peace of mind will have been worth all the toil and time. But even then, not all of the work that you do will make you jump for joy. Let's face it, there are lousy parts of every job. The fun and boring, good and bad parts all combine to make us the people we are. Everything we do, whether great or lousy, enriches us if we remain focused on our goals and pursuit of success. Don't worry about competing against others for what you hope to achieve. Instead, give deeper thought to the way that you compete with yourself.

We should all aspire to our own perceived standard of greatness. This standard is showcased by people we have observed, who have modeled this standard for us. Finding people we'd like to emulate gives us a plan for beginning our quest. But there's more to it than just that. By offering up our work as a tribute to the people who inspire us—and to God—we sow the seeds of love and gratitude that lead to transformational, positive development.

A Story to Tell

Without much fanfare, one of the greatest basketball players—and leaders—in sports history decided to hang up his hi-tops in 2016. No big announcement, no victory lap. Right in the middle of summer, when few people were paying attention, the great Tim Duncan left on his terms—the only way it was ever to be. He cared about three things: his teammates, winning, and the spirit of competition. Each one inspired the other. Everything else was secondary. Only a handful of athletes have ever exemplified the combination of selflessness, competitive greatness, hard work, and indomitable spirit that the great Tim Duncan did. He always delighted in finding a way to win, while delivering his best performance.

Tim Duncan was a leader of immeasurable impact: durable, humble, intelligent, consistent, and willing to put the team's best interests before his own. Day-to-day, consistency doesn't always stand out. But Duncan's consistency in performance is precisely what was so striking. His consistency was powered by his competitive drive. He committed to winning and making every player around him better. The way players like Duncan in basketball, Mariano Rivera in baseball, and Nicklas Lidström in hockey have carried themselves over their careers has raised the bar for competitive greatness: all class; an expectation of winning; a quiet confidence that they will come out on top.

Duncan's calm, genteel exterior belies a man who was one of the fiercest, most disciplined competitors the American sporting landscape ever witnessed. His extraordinary preparation, attention to detail, and desire to win were revered. Duncan exhibited those qualities as well as anyone to ever play the game. He demonstrated that competitive greatness requires two things we can always control: attitude and effort.

The crazy thing in life is that we don't always choose the sure thing. We want the flash, the slam dunk, the get-rich-quick scheme, the high-speed elevator to the top. Maybe someone has found it, but I'm convinced it doesn't exist. The Tim Duncan way, the consistently industrious, competitive way, is the one we should follow.

3 Questions on Competitive Greatness to Ask Yourself:

1. What are the methods and techniques you employ in developing your mindset for approaching everything you do?

2. Who are the role models you admire most?

3. What comes to mind when you think of competing with yourself?

Results of Competitive Greatness

> *I'm not in competition with anybody but myself. My goal is to beat my last performance." — Celine Dion*

Competitive greatness will lead you to the career and life you desire, once you mix this mindset with your enthusiasm and talents. In their *New York Times* bestseller, *Top Dog: The Science of Winning and Losing*, Po Bronson and Ashley Merryman use scientific analysis to determine what separates the winners from the losers. In an interview with NPR, Merryman asserts that a competitor's mindset geared toward winning makes a huge difference:

"And when you're playing to win you're thinking in sort of a big picture and you're looking for successes and how can you build on what you are doing right. ... And people who are playing not to lose are preventing mistakes. They're trying to stave off what they think is the eminent disaster in the things that work for them. ... But if you want to grow, if you want to challenge yourself, if you want to innovate, you have to force yourself to be playing to win." [6]

You don't need to be an athlete to challenge yourself. You have to *want it* badly enough to put forth your greatest effort, for the sake of producing the best result you are capable of. Competitive greatness is applicable to any student or business professional. It's applicable to any of us who make mistakes. Yes, that means all of us! We're all going to make mistakes. By making mistakes, we grow, learn how to innovate, and refine our approach. We turn adversity into our greatest teacher.

When you dedicate yourself to performing at your best, you'll earn supporters, build relationships, and win over many friends. Giving your very best, all the time, is a way of life. It requires that you think deeply and assess your abilities, so you can strengthen your strengths and gradually improve upon your weaknesses. Find *your* winner: the person in your personal and professional life whom you look up to. Observe this person's characteristics and behaviors, then try to emulate them. You'll find that the genius of competitive greatness comprises many practical values that are within your control.

I designate specific time each week to putting things in perspective and looking at my performance, in a multitude of areas, from a high-level view. I think we all need that for balance and to make sure our actions align with our mission. These are the times for us to re-evaluate why we're doing what we're doing.

Putting Things in Perspective

To demand more of ourselves, we also need to practice compassion in how we treat ourselves. We may have big goals, but if we're too tough on ourselves, we'll only get in our own way. That can lead to anger and envy, which are dangerous emotions that prevent us from being our best. Winners are able to persevere and utilize both good and bad emotions to their advantage as they perform. They channel any anxiety or fear by converting it into greater desire and energy. They use the love and respect they have for their loved ones, co-workers, or teammates as inspiration to keep moving forward, when every part of their mental and physical make-up tells them to stop.

Winners focus on results. Great athletes of yesteryear like Joe DiMaggio, and recent superstars like Tim Duncan cared deeply about what other people thought of their effort and performance. They cared because their preparation, concentration and effort in the moment meant everything to them.

President Theodore Roosevelt understood that to achieve what we truly want in life, we have to be in the arena competing. As he stated in one of his famous speeches:

It is not the critic who counts; not the man who points out how the strong man stumbles, or where the doer of deeds could have done them better. The credit belongs to the man who is actually in the arena, whose face is marred by dust and sweat and blood; who strives valiantly; who errs, who comes short again and again, because there is no effort without error and shortcoming; but who does actually strive to do the deeds; who knows great enthusiasms, the great devotions; who spends himself in a worthy cause; who at the best knows in the end the triumph of high achievement, and who at the worst, if he fails, at least fails while daring greatly, so that his place shall never be with those cold and timid souls who neither know victory nor defeat.[7]

When we're there in the arena, we become addicted to that feeling of leaving it all on the line—giving our all. We learn few rewards are greater than performing at our best. It's exhilarating.

Game Plan

1. Identify three areas of your life where you can improve. This could be your performance in school or how you approach each day at your job. Maybe there's a dream you keep on pushing off in the distance, for another day. Assess the current-state of each of these situations. Be honest. Validate this information with someone close to you that you trust. Then, begin putting together a "future-state" vision of what performing at your best would look like in each of these situations. Be specific! Once you have your future-state, begin at once to work toward making your vision a reality.

2. Think of the people you know personally that you have great respect for. Think of stars in their respective fields, whether it be business, technology or education. You'll find the common thread between these people is that they always perform at their best. Use these people as role models—a source of motivation and inspiration. They don't give up. So, why should you?

3. Focus on your mindset! Make a promise to compete each day to the best of your ability. It may be the way you take care of your infant child or teenager. Perhaps it's the preparation of studying for your nursing degree, software development certification, or how you train to get into the best shape of your life. Remember, it's a mindset first. How you treat others, the way you prepare, and how hard you work matters, from the smallest task to the largest. For you to perform at

your best when the "bright lights" are on, you must perform at your best when no one is watching.

Notes

[1] Coach Norman Dale, *Hoosiers*, directed by David Anspaugh, produced by Carter De Haven (1986; Helmdale Film Corp/Orion Productions).

[2] Competitive Greatness as defined by college basketball coaching great John Wooden from his "Pyramid of Success," available at http://www.atlanticleadershipgroup.com/images/stories/pyramidpdf%201500.jpg (accessed April 3, 2017).

[3] Joe DiMaggio, Source: The Sporting News (April 4, 1951), available at: http://www.baseball-almanac.com/quotes/quodimg.shtml

[4] John Wooden, Pyramid of Success, available at http://www.coachwooden.com/pyramid-of-success (accessed April 3, 2017).

[5] Pat Summitt, *Reach for the Summit: The Definite Dozen System for Succeeding at Whatever You Do* (New York: Broadway Books, 1998), 208.

[6] Po Bronson and Ashley Merryman, interview with Michel Martin, "The Science Of Being 'Top Dog,'" on *Tell Me More*, NPR, May 27, 2013, available at http://www.npr.org/2013/05/27/186479858/the-science-of-being-top-dog (accessed April 3, 2017).

[7] President Theodore Roosevelt, "The Man in the Arena," excerpt from "Citizenship in a Republic" speech, delivered at the Sorbonne, France, April 23, 1910.

CHAPTER 14

Hard Work

"There are no secrets to success. It is the result of prepara-tion, hard work, and learning from failure."

— *General Colin Powell (Ret.)*

DEFINITION:

Hard Work: Working intelligently and vigorously at a given task to complete it with maximum efficiency (my personal definition)

Industrious: constantly, regularly, or habitually active or occupied: diligent[1]

Growing up on the south shore of Long Island, my summer highlights consisted of going to the beach and attending basketball camp at Syracuse University. I'm a beach bum at heart, so sun and surf were always on my mind. When I wasn't at Long Beach, I was playing basketball, following in my brothers' footsteps and hoping to play in college.

Each year, my parents' big gift to us was one week at the Big Orange Basketball Camp, held on the Syracuse University campus, in the Carrier Dome. It was there we learned the game and developed our fundamental skills. Each day, a speaker came to address the campers after lunch. Syracuse legends, and sometimes Head Coach Jim Boeheim, came by to say, "Hello." The most memorable words I heard during those speeches came from former Syracuse player, Mike Hopkins.

"Hop" is now the head basketball coach at the University of Washington. In his playing days, he was known for his gritty, team-first approach and hustle. He knew the value of hard work and made that his calling card during his tenure with the program.

As he himself says, "I'm the guy that has kept working and working. Things have worked out for me."[2]

Coach Hopkins told us how he was lightly recruited out of high school in southern California. He told us he didn't have many college offers at all. He always needed to prove himself throughout every level of basketball. Then, he said words that have always stuck with me:

"When I got to Syracuse, I realized I wasn't good enough to play based on my talent alone. I asked myself, **"What does our team need?"** *I knew if I wanted to play, I had to do the things that other guys weren't willing to do: Dive on loose balls, get offensive rebounds, take charges and sacrifice my-self for the team. I had to be* **the hardest worker** *on the team. Hard work would be my meal ticket and how I would approach every practice and game."*

The SoCal kid fell in love with Syracuse and became a fan favorite. He earned the admiration of others for his hard work and great attitude. This approach has continued into his coaching. A "hard work" approach translates into any venture or medium. An industrious mindset of focusing on every detail may not come on most job descriptions, but it is an unwritten requirement. It's also a requirement for getting top grades in school. The list goes on. By exerting every drop of energy you have, with intelligence and dedication, you will benefit in any endeavor. In the basketball coaching profession, clichés abound. Here's one phrase that rings true in basketball and in life:

Hard work beats talent when talent doesn't work hard.

Mike Hopkins wasn't close to being the most talented player at Syracuse, but no one ever outworked him. He ended up becoming a starter during his four years in college because he worked hard and did what others weren't willing to do. Every basketball team needs a player like Mike Hopkins. Every school, hospital, company, and community needs one, too. Work hard. The world needs you.

The Core of Hard Work:

" *Hard work opens doors and shows the world that you are serious about being one of those rare—and special—human beings who use the fullness of their talents to do their very best." — Robin Sharma*

Mistakes and short-term failures are often the inspiration that lead to hard work. Hard work requires a commitment of time, planning, and a positive attitude. You can work hard at something all day long, but you won't make progress if your work is poorly planned and you hate what you do. When you endeavor to complete anything, it's imperative that you mentally, emotionally, and physically commit to working hard. Think of it as an official contract that you sign for yourself.

If you really want to make it official, put it in writing. This way, you commit it further to memory. Building a plan is a prerequisite that takes time, as is focusing on how you will spend your time. Ask anyone who's experienced a few of life's battles: time goes by quickly, and time will eat us alive if we choose to waste it.

Identify what it is that makes you happy. In fact, list all the things that make you happy. Know what you enjoy doing. Know what you don't. Then, work toward developing a schedule that plans most of your time around what you love—your strengths and passions. Take note of things people have complimented you on in the past. This will energize you to keep going.

All of us, at some point, are going to have responsibilities, errands, and obligations that we don't want to fulfill. I know. I'm right there with you. Hey, welcome to life! But we can't ignore these responsibilities. We must face them head on, with positive energy, and a willingness to do whatever it takes to get the job done. The more we practice this, the more we refine our approach to all our work. From there, we become more adept at identifying new opportunities and gravitating toward the work we love to do.

Everything first begins with an idea, which is given life when you have a *desire* to succeed and *belief* that you will. Think about your current situation: Whether you're a student, entrepreneur, working professional, or athlete, it's likely that you can identify several areas in your life where you can improve. Furthermore, if you're willing, I bet you not only have the desire,but that you're able to do the job that others will not. This takes sacrifice and hard work. It's a matter of aligning your mind, body, and spirit.

Find your thing. What you want can be yours, if you're willing to put in the work.

Obstacles to Living with Hard Work

- Laziness

- Excuses

- Cutting corners

- Giving up

- Thinking a half-hearted effort will cut it

What are you waiting for? What is delaying you from starting that project or "top priority" that you keep pushing off? Are you looking for a sign? Motivation or inspiration? Patience is a virtue, but being too patient is the sign of someone who's too fearful to begin. I know precisely how you feel. And guess what? So do the majority of human beings. We're black belts in wasting time. If they awarded a Nobel Prize for Procrastination, we'd receive the medal by unanimous vote. We humans tend to push things off and waste time. So, if it makes you feel any better, you have a community of support. Kind of.

Know this: procrastination leads to excuses. We don't recognize our excuses until we think introspectively about what we say and do. Under the microscope of our mind's eye, excuses tend to stand out. The longer we go on without doing this necessary thinking, the more excuses become a part of our repertoire. They come to define us. We should seek to destroy excuses like, "I don't have the time," "I'm not good enough," "I don't have enough experience," or "There's never an opportunity." That last one is my least favorite. There is an abundance of opportunities all around us. We just have to seek them out and find them.

I used to believe opportunities came along to certain people and not others. While it may seem that way, I ask you to dedicate time to researching the lives of people you admire. Study those who have become wildly successful. I think you'll find in many instances they came from nothing and created their own opportunities. They didn't wait around for opportunities to come to them. They worked hard to get them.

What are you putting off for tomorrow that you can do today?

Oprah Winfrey came from a broken family and was abused as a child. She kept powering forward, realizing that while she had talent, she needed to work twice as hard in a profession less friendly to minorities. J. K. Rowling wound up destitute and on the British equivalent of welfare. She kept writing. She literally worked her way out of despair and became one of the most successful authors in history. Martin Luther King Jr. could have let oppression and racism stand in the way of a future his predecessors only dreamed was possible. He got right out on the front lines, marching, influencing, and speaking his way to freedom for millions of people.

Do what you can, with what you have, where you are."— Theodore Roosevelt

President Theodore Roosevelt came from fantastic New York wealth. Teddy was a child of privilege. But ironically, the values we associate most with his life today are his extraordinary work ethic and his attitude—the vigor and love with which he lived his life. While Roosevelt benefited from opportunities as a child, he earned everything in his adult life. He wasn't handed anything. He wasn't one for making excuses. He made sacrifices, read voraciously, created new opportunities, and literally carved out the life that he envisioned in his dreams. He built himself up physically, spiritually, emotionally, and mentally, to ensure that no one would ever out-hustle him.

All of us will face obstacles in life. It could be a physical one, like asthma. It might be a reading impairment like dyslexia. Maybe it's poverty. These are the "barriers to entry" that threaten to derail us. They are the roadblocks that stand in our way. They will make or break us. But here's the secret: they begin in our minds! We can remove these barriers by conditioning our minds and training ourselves to give our best effort all the time.

3 Questions on Hard Work to Ask Yourself:

1. Am I giving my relationships, work, and goals the maximum amount of effort?

2. What is the one area of my life that requires the most focus and attention?

3. Am I willing to commit to improvement? Hard work is preceded by mental and emotional "buy-in"

Value within the Value

You might be reading this, thinking to yourself, I'm not the most educated, the fastest, or most experienced. Rest assured, neither am

I. And I'd like to think I'm doing just fine. Why? Because I'm living my dreams by emphasizing this fundamental ethos: I approach each situation positively and I work hard for what I set my mind to accomplish.

Achievement—both your sense of self-worth and the accomplishment of your goals—is earned through a positive, determined attitude and an uncompromising work ethic. Talent alone will only get you so far. Talent certainly helps. But I'd rather work with the individual who gives 100 percent effort every time, than with someone who only puts in effort part of the time. The industrious person is reliable, trustworthy, and very likely a team player.

Create your own opportunities by seeking them out and doing what others aren't willing to do. No one's going to give you anything. You have to work for it and earn it. Most successful people rise to the top, not because of a rich uncle or luck, but because of hard work and an opportunistic mindset. One of the finest Olympians in U.S. history is a prime example.

A Story to Tell

The incredible story of Olympic champion Wilma Rudolph[3] is one worth sharing for generations to come. Beyond her record-breaking athletic feats, what is most impressive about Rudolph is how she overcame stunning odds to compete in the first place. You see, giving up was never her thing. Rudolph was born a very sick child in 1940, premature and without much hope. She contracted polio, which led to infantile paralysis, which then caused her left leg to twist and grow abnormally. Throughout her youth she needed to get treatment on her leg. As she once described it: "My doctors told me I would never walk again. My mother told me I would. I believed my mother."

Rudolph also survived scarlet fever—at the time, a leading cause of death in children—and double pneumonia. She was the twentieth of twenty-two children and grew up poor in the segregated South. To say the deck was stacked against her would be an understatement of epic proportions. Just getting a chance on the field of competition seemed like a tall order. Yet as Ms. Rudolph proved, there is no substitute for hard work and a positive attitude. She persevered and played sports throughout her youth despite her ailments. She practiced every day and was so determined to succeed she simply powered her way out of leg braces and kept working until she was free.

" *Winning is great, sure, but if you are really going to do something in life, the secret is learning how to lose. Nobody goes undefeated all the time. If you can pick up after a crushing defeat, and go on to win again, you are going to be a champion someday." — Wilma Rudolph*

She first medaled at the Olympics when she was only sixteen years old. She reached the pinnacle of her sport four years later at the age of twenty. She was the first female American to win three gold medals, doing so at the Rome Olympic Games in 1960. Rudolph relied on hard work to become one of the greatest female athletes in history. She refused to let any internal or external limitations stop her. She's a true hero and example that hard work pays off, no matter how challenging our circumstances.

Luck

None of us make it on our own, though we do attract greater energy and synergy from the universe when we're putting forth positive thoughts and actions. We have a positive force behind us when we're working hard for something we deeply desire and believe in. Perhaps you've seen the famous rejection letter sent to Paul Hewson, better known as Bono, from one of the most successful music groups of all time, U2. I've included it here:

10th May 1979,

Dear Mr. Hewson,

Thank you for submitting your tape of 'U2' to RSO, we have listened with careful consideration, but feel it is not suitable for us at present.

We wish you luck with your future career.

Yours sincerely,

ALEXANDER SINCLAIR[4]

We can surmise that not too long after, Mr. Sinclair probably would have agreed that U2's tape was suitable for RSO Records! Sinclair ended up fueling the motivation of a young Irishman and his bandmates to work harder than they ever had. Paul Hewson, Edge, and the boys were determined to defy probability and the odds against them. In becoming one of the biggest bands in the world, U2 showed that hard work pays off.

When we think of how slim the odds are of reaching spectacular levels of success, we tend to react in one of two ways: we either meet the challenge head-on and give all we have, or we retreat in fear and start making excuses. The people who retreat in fear and make excuses are the same ones who will tell you the success of U2 or others was simply luck. They can't fathom how or why they got the breaks. Luck exists, but it's not what we think. We create our own luck by working hard and backing our dreams with faith and a positive attitude. There's a famous saying you've probably heard before, "The harder I work, the luckier I get." Keep this in mind when you think about what you want to become in life.

Results of Hard Work

" *There may be people that have more talent than you, but there's no excuse for anyone to work harder than you."—Derek Jeter*

I met recently with a young woman who was paralyzed from the waist down in a terrible motorcycle accident. She told me that she could have given up and succumbed to the reality of her situation. She experienced anger, frustration and disappointment when she was told she'd never walk again. She realized, if she wanted to move on with her life, she had a choice to make: work hard every day to make her life a masterpiece, or give in to fear and anger. She chose to give life her all. Despite her setback, she's continuing her education to become a medical doctor. She's one of the most positive, upbeat people I've ever met. She simply will not be denied. She understands what it means to work hard and she's willing to put in the effort to reap the results.

Hard work defines who we are. It shapes how we are perceived by our peers in the classroom, on athletic fields and in the workplace. A person with a "by any means necessary" attitude is going to conquer any assignment put in front of her. That person won't accept excuses. Hardworking people find a way to succeed on an algebra exam, even when math is not their strong suit. They teach others to overcome what holds them back. They find people who can help them in the areas where they are deficient. They are resourceful and efficient with the use of their time and energy.

Show me a parent, athlete, student, teacher, or scientist who works hard, and I'll show you someone who's going to find—likely sooner rather than later—success in their given craft. Hard work attracts and inspires winners. Hard work cuts through alibis, excuses, and procrastination. It's unwilling to accept second best. Work hard and work intelligently, whatever your circumstances are. Make hard work your meal ticket. It's your choice. We hear a lot about productivity these days. Productivity is driven by hard work and a positive attitude. This requires you to focus with maximum energy, attention, and efficiency on what you have in front of you in that moment. Make no mistake, everything begins right there.

Take the example of the greatest basketball player this world has ever seen: Michael Jordan. He was cut from his high school varsity basketball team while a sophomore at Laney HS in Wilmington, NC. He played at the junior varsity level that season and dominated, but did not join the varsity team until his junior year. Incredible, yes, as it's a wonder the Laney HS boys varsity basketball coach kept his job! The bigger picture is part of the mystique of why Jordan became the player he did.

Being told he wasn't good enough for varsity inspired Jordan to work harder than ever before. He practiced for several hours every day, all throughout the year, and used this experience as the turning point of his life. Jordan owned hard work like few people ever have. He willed himself into becoming the best. He played with a burning desire, showing a **fire** for basketball that fueled his rise to the top of the game, as you'll see in the next chapter.

Game Plan

1. Hard work is not just a practice or action. It begins as a state of mind. To intelligently work on something with your best effort, you must be willing to make a promise to yourself. This means eliminating other worthy options, as well as distractions. Make your decision based on the information at hand. Then, go full-throttle with your best effort.

2. Pay close attention to detail and "the little things." The "little things" are the often-ignored steps in the process that make a big difference. For example, if you want to open your own coffee shop, you need a well-rounded approach toward business. It's not just about brewing great coffee. You'll need to recruit reliable staff, manage them well, market your business and listen to what your customer wants! Hard, intelligent work requires you to focus on every part of what you do, from the purchase of the physical location, to the equipment that brews your coffee.

3. Stop making excuses. Eliminate them from your thoughts. Remove them from your vocabulary! Once you stop making excuses, you eliminate the option of quitting. You stop

doubting yourself. Hard work is the end-result of belief in yourself and a positive attitude, which is backed by persistence and perseverance. Hard work and perseverance eliminate excuses.

Notes

[1] "Industrious," *Merriam-Webster*,
https://www.merriam-webster.com/dictionary/industriousness (accessed May 21, 2017).

[2] Mike Hopkins, quoted in Mark Medina, "Syracuse assistance, former Mater Dei standout Mike Hopkins overcomes the odds," *Los Angeles Daily News*, August 20, 2016, http://www.dailynews.com/events/20160820/syracuse-assistant-former-mater-dei-standout-mike-hopkins-overcomes-the-odds (accessed May 21, 2017).

[3] M.B. Roberts, "Rudolph ran and world went wild," ESPN Sports Century, https://espn.go.com/sportscentury/features/00016444.html (accessed May 21, 2017).

[4] "Read U2's Rejection Letter From A Record Label In 1979," Huffington Post, March 7, 2014, http://www.huffingtonpost.com/2014/03/07/u2-rejection-letter_n_4920625.html (accessed May 21, 2017).

CHAPTER 15

Fire

"Be who God meant you to be, and you will set the world on fire."

—St. Catherine of Siena

<u>**DEFINITION:**</u>

Burning passion: ardor; liveliness of imagination: inspiration [1]

Michael Jordan came into the NBA in the fall of 1984, a wide-eyed, 21-year-old from the University of North Carolina. His otherworldly athleticism and raw talent caught the eye of millions during his college days. Arriving in "the league" meant it was his opportunity to prove himself against the best players in the world. Jordan didn't dominate immediately. But before long, it was clear that the future of the NBA was the man wearing #23 for the Chicago Bulls.

Jordan went on to phenomenal scoring and individual achievements throughout the remainder of the 1980s, but each season, the Bulls weren't good enough to make the NBA Finals. A world championship seemed far off. It's easy to forget now, because to every sports fan and non-sports fan alike, Jordan is revered, not just as a great player, but as the ultimate champion. Just remember this: Jordan did not win an NBA Championship until his seventh season in the league. It took blood, sweat, tears, thousands of hours in the gym, and a ferocious enthusiasm for the game of basketball to finally lift him to the exalted status of world champion.

" *I will not let anything get in the way of me and my competitive enthusiasm to win."— Michael Jordan*

The story of Michael Jordan is chock full of lessons about hard work, desire, positive attitude, and overcoming adversity. Jordan's secret to success throughout his legendary career was not his Air Jordan sneakers (but boy were they awesome!), nor his signature move of sticking out his tongue while he drove to the basket. Rather, Jordan's greatness and "extra gear" was the fire with which he prepared, practiced, and conditioned his mind. This translated into the way he played the game.

Jordan was beaten down by the great Boston Celtics and Detroit Pistons teams of the 1980s, but along the way, he kept strengthening his belief. He burned with unquenchable fire that willed the most out of himself and his teammates. He possessed an indomitable will mixed with determined persistence in approach. Jordan had all the physical talent in the world. But he became a legend by outworking, outhustling, and overpowering his competitors with his *mental approach* to the game. Michael Jordan played with a fire that few other athletes ever have. He simply would not be denied. Jordan ensured that his physical skills matched his mental, emotional, and spiritual development.

This combination of talents and drive led him to six championships, and his place in history as one of the greatest athletes who ever lived.

At any given moment in time, we are exactly what our natural talents and skills are. The great differentiator is what I refer to as "fire." Fire is that *je ne sais quoi* or difficult-to-explain quality that you only know when you see it. And you want it for yourself, because it will add color and meaning to your life, like few values can.

We can look to Michael Jordan as an extraordinary example of someone who summoned the fire from within to self-motivate and transform his mind to match his brilliant physical talents. We may not have his hops or jump shot, but we all can energize ourselves with enthusiasm the way Jordan did. Fire will help us soar—even if not quite at the altitude that His Airness did.

The Core of Fire

> *The world is ruled, and the destiny of civilization is established, by the human emotions. People are influenced in their actions, not by reason so much as by 'feelings.' The creative faculty of the mind is set into action entirely by emotions."[2]— Napoleon Hill*

Fire is the feeling that makes you want to scream out the lyrics to your favorite song while riding on a coastal highway, even when you catch people looking. Maybe you're blasting Colbie Caillat or Bruno Mars, but I'm pumping Foo Fighters through those speakers!

Fire is the value of maximum attitude, passion, and effort coalescing to form a fusion of output that elevates you to a highly productive, highly confident level. It's a characteristic that can be cultivated, enhanced, and self-coached, if our willpower and minds are welcoming and ready. Fire is a feeling of burning passion for that which you desire and believe to be pure. It will lift you from the doldrums of anxiety, fear, and worry into the light of belief, joy, and victory. It's in this state of mind that our most fertile thoughts arise. It's a form of mental rehabilitation that we can perform on ourselves.

Fire elevates our thinking, encouraging and enabling us to rise to challenges while persevering through difficult times. Self-motivation is a necessary, though undervalued tool. Too often, we rely on others to motivate us. But what happens when our workout buddy suddenly stops showing up to the gym? Or when our friend finds some French hunk named Jacques who sweeps her off her feet, robbing us of our study partner? What then?!

It's great when others are there to motivate us. And when we can help to enhance and inspire someone's burning passion, we have aided them beyond measure. But we can't bank on someone else being there to motivate us, any more than we can trust that the stock market won't crash. And honestly, others can't always count on us being there to motivate them, no matter how much we may want to be, because that's just not always possible. We must look within at the boldness of our human spirit.

Continue to let your light—your fire—shine through to guide you. Know this, my friend—the flame can be fanned by observing and watching others, but you must rely on your interior power to cultivate and produce enthusiasm. Fire is the passion that speaks to our soul, soothes it, and makes us want more. It's as fleeting as we want it to be, and as everlasting as the light inside all of us.

Obstacles to Living with Fire

" *Success is stumbling from failure to failure with no loss of enthusiasm."— Winston Churchill*

- Apathy

- Negative mindset due to failure(s)

- Lack of awareness or knowledge of this special power

- Lack of initiative/planning

We all know that life sometimes deals us a difficult hand. In those moments, it's the power to keep moving forward that we summon to help us. The main obstacles to fire are apathy and a negative outlook due to previous failures or mistakes. Life is incredibly hard when we don't care or when we lack excitement about living. We need fire to color our lives and help us rise above mediocrity and unpleasant circumstances.

Where do you get your motivation from? My motivation comes from the fire inside of me, the indescribable power that fuels my dreams and inner creativity. This power has led me to personal freedom, greater clarity of thought and renewed energy for living each day with purpose. I can assure you, all fire requires is a willingness to believe, and the desire to get to the core of what inspires you.

Introspection and deep, personal reflection are key to living a life of freedom. So are finding positive, motivational resources like books, videos, and empowering speeches that help illuminate our souls and give us cause to fight on for what we want. These resources help us to analyze our experiences and thoughts, providing us with a greater sense of direction and purpose.

Fire, when channeled and integrated into our daily routine, helps to combat apathy. It leads us to take the initiative to plan our day and become more self-aware. This motivational boost is so important for success. Fire inspires you to live each day with a smile on your face. If you find yourself doubting your motives or living in negativity, find something to get fired up about. Think positive thoughts about things that bring you joy and ignite the passion inside of you.

Value within the Value

> *A small body of determined spirits fired by an unquenchable faith in their mission can alter the course of history."*— Mahatma Gandhi

Finding Forrester is one of my favorite movies because it speaks to who I am, what I want to be, and the people I desire to help. It's an inspirational tale of a young man who discovers his writing talent, thanks to a curmudgeonly, reclusive writer. Say what?! Yes, that is the magic of Hollywood and, indeed, the magic of life. I coached high school basketball in New York City for three years, where the movie takes place, so the plot resonates deeply with me. Helping young men—and women—reach their potential on and off the basketball court is one of the key missions of my life.

Sean Connery plays the role of William Forrester, a character very similar to the real-life reclusive author J. D. Salinger, famous for his novel, *The Catcher in the Rye*. In "the winter of his life," as he says at the movie's climax, Connery stumbles upon a promising African-

American teenager from the Bronx named Jamal Wallace. Wallace, portrayed by the superb Rob Brown, is a rising scholastic basketball star at the fictional Mailer Callow school—a school similar to ones I coached against.

The improbable, remarkable nature of their relationship—and common bond of writing—is the glue that holds this film together. Mix that with their similarities of stubbornness and hesitancy to trust others, and you have a striking combination. In his magnificent, charming Bronx apartment, Forrester helps Wallace find his purpose in life by imploring and instructing him to find his writing voice through a series of unconventional, life-changing lessons.

Revisiting this film makes me realize that writing speaks to me in a way few other mediums can. *This is my passion!* What is your passion? I ask because I believe it's one of the most important questions in life. What is the kindling that stokes the fire inside of you? Once you find it, it will continue to fuel what you love and carry you throughout your life. You can cultivate this by continuing to pursue activities for which you have love and skills. Place your energy, time, and resources into doing things that bring out the fire in you. It may become your paid job; it may only be a hobby or a side gig. It may be the time you get to spend each day with your son, daughter, or friends. It may be using your creative imagination to design something never seen before.

We owe it to ourselves to tap into this power, which is of great magnitude and light, that can guide us, invigorate us, and bring greater meaning to our journey. Coach Kevin Eastman said it best: "It takes three things to be a 'special' player: talent, character, and competitive fire."

You don't need to be the most talented to be the best at what you do. You need to combine your talent with a positive attitude, infused by intensity and passion. Everyone respects an individual with a passion for life that says, "I love what I do, and I do it with zeal."

A Poem

If you desire to live with a burning passion for life, and to forge your own path, then this poem by Irish novelist and poet Oscar Wilde is for you:

THE ARTIST

ONE evening there came into his soul the desire to fashion an image of The Pleasure that Abideth for a Moment. And he went forth into the world to look for bronze. For he could think only in bronze.

But all the bronze of the whole world had disappeared, nor anywhere in the whole world was there any bronze to be found, save only the bronze of the image of The Sorrow that Endureth For Ever.

Now this image he had himself, and with his own hands, fashioned, and had set it on the tomb of the one thing he had loved in life. On the tomb of the dead thing he had most loved had he set this image of his own fashioning, that it might serve as a sign of the love of man that dieth not, and a symbol of the sorrow of man that endureth for ever. And in the whole world there was no other bronze save the bronze of this image.

And he took the image he had fashioned, and set it in a great furnace, and gave it to the fire. And out of the bronze of the image of The Sorrow that Endureth For Ever he fashioned an image of The Pleasure that Abideth for a Moment.

Find a way to keep going. That's the meaning of these beautiful words. Find a way when others don't think you can and you don't think you can. Find a way. We were created to live boldly and do amazing things. We can and will if we keep going. The respect and admiration of our peers is instrumental in giving life to our belief in ourselves and the positive emotions that accompany it. But we must be the ones we rely on most to energize ourselves. We must summon the passion—the fire—to keep going even when there is no bronze left. Even when it means reinventing something we've already created. Or better yet, reinventing ourselves.

Results of Fire

Your task is clear: Find what motivates you. Find those activities that give you the chills and enable you to respond in the most positive ways. Find what lifts your spirit, empowering you to believe that what you formerly thought to be impossible is most definitely possible. Harness this energy, and burn with desire that will not be denied.

Go back to the well, where you find joy in your heart. You may find your motivation to be music, sports, technology, nature, or the smile of someone you admire. Meditate on these feelings. Replicate and summon them every day, to bring a greater joy and feeling of purpose to your life. Use this power to your advantage, for your betterment and the attainment of your dreams and goals.

When you were a kid, what did you dream of being when you grew up? Maybe you wanted to be a fireman or woman, astronaut, librarian, lawyer, doctor or professional athlete. If you haven't ended up in one of these lofty professions, that doesn't mean complacency should set in. Don't feel like you've failed, because you haven't. This is your time to dig-in a bit deeper and start formulating your game plan. This all begins with an idea and a burning desire. You can always choose to stoke the fire inside of you. You always have that power.

As I've grown, I've learned that those priceless seeds of optimism and imagination should charge a lifelong journey toward living with enthusiasm and purpose. When my mind is occupied with enthusiasm for what I do, I feel unstoppable. It's why I took the time seven years ago to write down all the things I wanted in my life. I didn't do this to become rich or (necessarily) more successful.

I did it because it dawned on me that so much of the enthusiasm that filled my life throughout my youth and into my twenties had suddenly vanished. I wasn't doing what I loved. My motivations were dormant. It was slowly killing me inside. I had to make a change, and by God, I did. I now do things I love to do—things that draw on my true talents that bring out the best in me. Maybe you feel the same.

Enthusiasm is the secret formula that gives life to every goal we aim to accomplish. In his popular book, *Enthusiasm Makes the Difference*, Norman Vincent Peale quotes Arnold Toynbee, who once said,

"Enthusiasm can only be aroused by two things; first, an ideal which takes the imagination by storm, and second, a definite intelligible plan for a carrying that ideal into practice." [3]

There's a fire inside all of us. We've been given the match to light it. We can if we simply tap into our inner strength. When your thoughts are vibrating at high intensity, you get excited. You burn to achieve the object of your desire. Let the fire and adrenaline inside of you stir up the passion you need to transform your ideas into reality. Follow your heart to where it is leading you, then put together a plan for living a life that incorporates what you love into how you can support yourself. Life is so much more fulfilling when you do what you love.

Game Plan

1. Determine what your biggest interests are. Narrow them down to just one or two things. Those things are your passion(s). Your passion should make you feel like you're "in the zone." When you're thinking of this passion or doing this thing, it should ignite the fire inside your soul and give you an extra boost. It may be something you've done in the past. It could be something you think about and do right now. Frame it up and start putting time and energy into your passion.

2. Practice continuous learning. Here's an example: I love the game of basketball. I played high school and college basketball and I've watched thousands of basketball games. But when I got into coaching, I knew I needed to get back to

basics. I read books. I read through old playbooks. I attended coaching clinics and recorded interviews on TV. I studied videos on YouTube. I asked thousands of questions to my fellow coaches and even players. I couldn't get enough. Your passion may be acting, playing the guitar or maybe it's cars. Keep stoking your fire by learning more about these subjects. Become an expert. In the process, you'll cultivate a desirable skill that will benefit you.

Notes

[1] *"Enthusiasm," Merriam-Webster,*

https://www.merriam-webster.com/dictionary/fire *(accessed May 15, 2017).*

[2] *Napoleon Hill, Think and Grow Rich.*

[3] *Norman Vincent Peale, Enthusiasm Makes the Difference, quoting Arnold Toynbee (Fireside, 1967), 8.*

CHAPTER 16

Courage

"One isn't necessarily born with courage, but one is born with potential. Without courage, we cannot practice any other virtue with consistency. We can't be kind, true, merciful, generous, or honest." [1]

— *Maya Angelou*

DEFINITION:

Mental or moral strength to venture, persevere, and withstand danger, fear, or difficulty [2]

Many of us may live our whole lives without knowing how we would react in a moment of life-threatening danger. Others, like Dr. Liviu Librescu, are called to react in times of incomprehensible evil. Dr. Librescu was a Holocaust survivor and highly accomplished scientist who worked as a professor at Virginia Tech University for twenty-two years. He was on campus, teaching, on the morning of April 16, 2007, when the terrifying Virginia Tech massacre occurred, which killed thirty-two people.

Librescu was just a boy when the Nazis invaded Romania.[3] They sent him and thousands of Romanian men to hard labor camps. He made it through the brutal war and went on to study aerospace engineering at the Polytechnic University of Bucharest. After working as a researcher for more than twenty years, Librescu was forced out of academia and fired from his job for refusing to swear allegiance to the Communist Party of Romania. Thanks to an intervention by then-Israeli Prime Minister Menachem Begin, Librescu and his family immigrated to Israel.

He wouldn't arrive in Blacksburg, Virginia, until 1985. It was there he stayed until the morning of his death, when he faced yet another moment that would define his heroic life. Librescu heard gunfire from the neighboring classroom where he was teaching. He peeked out and could see the gunman, Seung-Hui Cho, who was in the midst of his shooting rampage. Librescu immediately sprang into action. He locked the door to his classroom and held the doors shut, serving as a human shield. He ordered his students to escape through the classroom window to safety outside.

Librescu saved the lives of twenty-two students in his classroom that day; sadly, one student did lose his life. The only other life lost was Librescu's. Shaped by the atrocities of the Holocaust, Librescu was a lifelong survivor and a brave, thoughtful leader. When he sensed danger, he decided to face it with undaunted courage, quickly assessing the situation. He determined that it was his duty to save the lives of the students in his classroom. He could have fled the room and left with his students, but he stayed. He blocked the door with his own body. There was no fear in Dr. Liviu Librescu—only pure courage.

The Core of Courage

Courage comes in many forms. Courage can be words delivered at peril to a speaker, in defiance of tyranny. Courage can be the action that directly influences a situation to save others, such as in the case of Dr. Liviu Librescu. Above all, the value of courage requires that we make a fundamental decision to do what is essential to living: **Risk**.

To live is to risk.

To risk means to give—or potentially give up—something in exchange for the gain or betterment of others or yourself. Risk also means that we potentially give or give up something without any promise that we'll gain anything back. We can't live with a "Poor Thinker's" mindset. In other words, if we think we'll never do great things, then it's as sure as 1+1 = 2 that we won't. We'll never even act. Finding personal fulfillment and joy from our life's work requires risk!

Begin to put things in motion. Be brave! The output of living courageously is the realization that a life we've imagined to be worth living, is in fact worth living. The best bet in life is always the one we place on ourselves.

Courage may be summoned literally in seconds. Still, as Captain Chesley "Sully" Sullenberger[4] would tell you, courage is an accumulation of thought about how we will act: "We all have heard about ordinary people who find themselves in extraordinary situations. They act courageously or responsibly, and their efforts are described as if they opted to act that way on the spur of the moment ... I believe many people in those situations actually have made decisions years before." [5]

Courage and risk are intertwined, and taking a chance is a big part of living. We may not know in advance when to act with courage, but knowing what it means to be courageous shapes our current and future moments.

Obstacle to Living with Courage

> *I learned that courage was not the absence of fear, but the triumph over it. The brave man is not he who does not feel afraid, but he who conquers that fear."—Nelson Mandela*

- Fear

Fear of Success

It's time we take a closer look at fear—after all, the value of courage is all about how we both withstand and conquer this mighty adversary. Or is it a friend?

In theory, it seems foolish to fear success—to fear the life we desire. In practice, fear of success is often what holds us back from achieving our dreams. As a mentor once told me, "What's in the way, is the way." To become successful, we're going to have to conquer fear. We're going to have to discover our true selves on the journey. Once we do, we can't be afraid to show others. Most people won't label it as such, but the fear of revealing our true selves to the world is a disease. When we view it in those terms, it helps us to diagnose the problem. Then crush it.

I used to be afraid of sharing my true self with friends and loved ones—so imagine how much harder it was to do so with perfect strangers. I found over time that this fear, not the fear of failure, is what was holding me back. Does that sound like you? This is what fear of acceptance and success looks like:

- Fear of posting your art, writing, or feelings in the public sphere, whether via social media or in person, due to a fear of criticism

- Fear of telling someone how much you care about them ... that you love them ... that they mean something to you

- Fear of giving someone a compliment or looking to build a personal or professional relationship because you don't know if you'll be acknowledged

- Feeling you may not be "worthy" or equipped to handle success; uncertainty around receiving praise and recognition

If you're a writer, keep writing and finding ways to improve, even after you've sold the first thousand copies of your book. If you're working your way up in the business world, find your clear path to promotion. Don't be afraid to tell people what you want. Find out what it takes to get there and exceed those requirements. If you're in a relationship at a crossroads, don't be afraid to love someone so much, that you let them go.

It takes a lot of courage to put ourselves out there, to represent our emotions, feelings, and who we are in the exact way that we want. There are countless ways for us to doubt ourselves: *What will we say? How will we perform? What if the conditions aren't what we expected? What if the competition is better than we thought?* What if I inundate myself with even more questions?!

I think back to when I was in sixth grade and I was sweating bullets, crippled by fear about what I might say to the girl that I wanted to ask out. I didn't have any plan, all I knew was that I found her attractive. During the night of the college basketball national championship game, I was amped up, so I mustered up the courage to finally call and ask her out. She said, "Yes." The exhilaration was incredible.

It was in that moment—approximately 1.38 painstaking seconds that felt like an eternity—when I realized that I wasn't afraid of whether the answer would be "Yes" or "No." I was only afraid of the anticipation: mustering up the courage to say the words and to act upon what I imagined. Not sure about you, but that anticipation is what *used to* hold me back. I've learned every great achievement or feeling of self-satisfaction comes from overcoming some kind of fear. Overcoming fear is about believing in yourself and not fretting over the outcome. There's no reason to worry when you believe in your decisions.

66 *Our deepest fear is not that we are inadequate. Our deepest fear is that we are powerful beyond measure. It is our Light, not our Darkness, that most frightens us."— Marianne Williamson, Return to Love*

We don't respect ourselves or give ourselves enough credit when we doubt and live in fear about future outcomes. This is directly rooted in a lack of faith. We can drive success and move mountains when we choose faith and reject the fear of success. Fear is both our friend and our enemy. When we're weak mentally, spiritually, and emotionally, fear is poison. It will destroy us. When we're strong in these areas, and we feel capable and confident in our abilities, fear can be a catalyst that drives us to a potential that we may have previously thought was unachievable.

This is a discomforting thought for some, yet it can become an empowering realization: we're vulnerable creatures. We're driven by emotions. This is why a constantly improving mindset toward emotional intelligence is imperative, and why a values-based foundation positions us for success. When we overcome the fear of success and acceptance, we grow more confident. We become more persistent, resolute, and hungry for our goals. Some people may perceive this as cockiness or arrogance. Let that be their problem, not yours.

There's so much that we're afraid of, which means there's so much to overcome. When we gain clarity, we realize that most fear is a waste of time. The fear of success prevents us from living the life we want. The quicker you confront this, the sooner you begin to take control of a life that was always yours in the first place.

Fear of Failure

Let me begin by first defining what fear of failure means. Actually, I'll leave that to the folks at *Mind Tools*. Their definition provides a great framework that we can work from: "fear of failure (also called 'atychiphobia') is when we allow that fear to stop us from doing the things that can move us forward to achieve our goals."[6]

Moving forward. Achieving goals. Isn't that what we want? Think about it—have you ever made progress when you've dwelled too much in the past? So, why do we let the fear of failure stop us in our tracks? In my personal experience, I've found it often comes down to three things:

- We fear what others might think of us (social reaction)

- We fear that which we desire most (over-obsessing)

- We convince ourselves that we can't do something that we really can (lack of confidence)

We should care what others think—up to a point. Because only we control our direction in life. The decisions we make, relationships we enter, and activities we participate in are all within our power. That which we choose, we also have to live with. Failure will only ever define us negatively if we allow it. We should aim to let it define us positively by embracing it once it occurs. This is where I differ from the above definition of fear of failure. I believe the fear of failure can induce courage! Instead of letting it stop us in our tracks, why not convert that adversity into an advantage? We can use challenging moments as turning points that embolden our spirit.

Once we do, we can work on building toward something better—something transformational. That may be the courage to ask out the man you've always wanted to meet. It could be trying out for a play or taking an acting class. It may simply be removing the biggest potential roadblock to achieving your dream: yourself.

Fear of failure can serve as a great motivator to improve our situation by refusing to accept the status quo. Steve Jobs was fired from the company that he started (Apple)!! So, what did he do?

Instead of letting fear sink him, he let it drive him. He founded a multi-million dollar company, NeXT. Then, he played a major role as top shareholder at computer animation film studio, Pixar. He returned to Apple ten years later, became CEO, and transformed Apple from a company on the brink of bankruptcy to the most profitable company in the world. See, fear can be a good thing!

> " *Tell your heart that the fear of suffering is worse than the suffering itself. And that no heart has ever suffered when it goes in search of its dreams, because every second of the search is a second's encounter with God and with eternity."— Paulo Coehlo, The Alchemist*

For those of us who refuse to give in or give up, we know we have the choice to embrace our situations or run from them. Running away is a telltale sign of succumbing to fear. Running away from our problems only prolongs the inevitable. It also hurts our prospects for future success. If we never confront fear, we'll continue to run away when the going gets tough. Unless we correct our course, we'll never know what it's like to overcome adversity and failure. Whether you fear failing a job interview, or taking the first step on your side-project, when you run away and give up, you lose.

Value within the Value

Sometimes, we run away from things when we sense they're too hard. We think it requires too much effort. We ask ourselves questions like: "Am I up to the task?" "Do I want to go through with all the steps and work that will lead to a positive result or outcome?" Those questions run through our mind. It's courage that carries us forward, willing us in the direction where our heart desires to lead us.

Sure, a fear of failure can lead us to doubt our abilities, but I've found the greatest damage to our psyche is more the social perception than the internalized emotion. This is why risk-taking is imperative. Writer Bill Blankschaen says, "Calculated risks fuel our growth when we step out from where we are to where we want to be. There is no sure thing in leadership—except the consequences of standing still."[7]   Courage eliminates the fear of standing still, that lifelong foe otherwise known as "indecision."

A Story to Tell

You might be familiar with the story of a young Ronald Reagan and the cobbler who sold him shoes. When he was a boy, the future president of the United States went to a cobbler to get fitted for a pair of shoes. Back then, it was not like it is today when you show up at the mall—or peruse online—and have your pick of what you want. You had to be sized.

The cobbler asked Reagan what type of shoes he wanted. He replied, "I don't know." The cobbler asked him about the color and the shape of the toes—flat or round—and again Reagan responded, "I don't know." So, the cobbler went on to make the shoes, and to prove a point, he made two completely different shoes. One was black, the other brown. Each shoe had a different toe. When Reagan came to collect his shoes and pay the cobbler, he asked why in the world he made a mismatched set of shoes. The cobbler replied, "If you do not make your own decisions, somebody else will make them for you."

Knowing what you want requires focus, skill, and discipline. Knowing what you want necessitates that you reflect on things— even the type of shoes you want. When you don't know what you want, it's easier to fear the unknown. When you know what you want, even if you fear failing, you're more likely to embrace the moment, because you have a road map and the courage to follow it to the right destination. Hopefully, somewhere where your GPS still works!

Results of Courage

> *I want to be in the arena. I want to be brave with my life. And when we make the choice to dare greatly, we sign up to get our asses kicked. We can choose courage or we can choose comfort, but we can't have both. Not at the same time. Vulnerability is not winning or losing; it's having the courage to show up and be seen when we have no control over the outcome. Vulnerability is not weakness; it's our greatest measure of courage."— Brené Brown Rising Strong: The Reckoning, the Rumble, the Revolution*

Here's the cold, hard truth: we're all going to fail. We're going to make mistakes in our personal relationships, jobs, in the pursuit of our dreams, and in things we say or do. We're all going to encounter the adversity that comes from failing. We're going to get knocked down. Check that ... we're all going to get knocked on our butts. The question is, will we have the courage to pick ourselves back up? To those who answer "Yes!" you know that this is the mindset of a champion. This is when you refuse to accept defeat. The fear of failure, when used to our advantage, steels our mind against losing.

It's in that moment that we commit to getting back up and trying again.

We remember giants like Dr. Martin Luther King Jr., who gave his all to fighting for the freedom and civil rights of African-Americans. Dr. King risked his life—and later lost his life—by leading and participating in peaceful protests and marches. He organized and mobilized people to stand up and fight for freedom and liberty they never had. The result of Dr. King's work is equality today for African-Americans that may never have been achieved. His courageous vision led to powerful actions that caused the leaders of this country and citizens of the world to notice. I'll finish this chapter with his powerful words:

"Courage is an inner resolution to go forward despite obstacles; cowardice is submissive surrender to circumstances. Courage breeds creativity; cowardice represses fear and is mastered by it."

Game Plan

1. Do what is in your heart—that which is pure and derived from how you truly feel. We all play mind games with ourselves, wondering if the wishes and desires of our heart are true. Stop doubting and questioning. Sometimes, it's good to be more impulsive. Listen to your heart. Then, fine-tune this in synchronization with what is in your mind. To be courageous, you have to lead with your heart!

2. Ask yourself these two questions: What is the cost of living in fear? And, what is the cost of not saying or acting upon something because of the silly fear of what others might think? I think you'll find the cost for both of those things is prohibitive. When you don't say what you want or when you don't move, you stay right where you are, indecisive and scared. Courageous people stand up for what's right and take action.

3. What you speak over your life will become your reality if you dedicate yourself to backing up your words through actions. This requires planning, concentration, commitment, and hard work. Once you do these things, the answer of whether you should stay silent or act with courage will be plain for you to see.

Notes

[1] Maya Angelou, from an interview in *USA Today*, March 5, 1988.

[2] "Courage," *Merriam-Webster*, https://www.merriam-webster.com/dictionary/courage (accessed March 14, 2017).

[3] Watch: "Virginia Tech—Courage Under Fire," www.ncfje.org via YouTube, https://www.youtube.com/watch?v=tEHm64RnjAs (accessed March 11, 2017)

[4] Captain Chesley "Sully" Sullenberger is the former US Airlines pilot, who saved the lives of everyone on board his plane on January 15, 2009, when he safely executed an emergency landing in the Hudson River.

[5] Captain Chesley "Sully" Sullenberger, *Highest Duty: My Search for What Really Matters* (William Morrow, October 13, 2009), 153.

[6] Mind Tools Editorial Team, "Overcoming Fear of Failure: Facing Fears and Moving Forward," Mind Tools, https://www.mindtools.com/pages/article/fear-of-failure.htm (accessed April 5, 2017).

[7] Bill Blankschaen, "Fear of Failure: Why It's Essential to Success," SkipPrichard Leadership Insights, https://www.skipprichard.com/fear-of-failure-why-its-essential-to-success/#close (accessed April 5, 2017).

CHAPTER 17

Perseverance

"Permanence, perseverance, and persistence in spite of all obstacles, discouragements, and impossibilities: It is this, that in all things distinguishes the strong soul from the weak."

— *Thomas Carlyle*

DEFINITION:

Continued effort to do or achieve something despite difficulties, failure, or opposition: the action or condition or an instance of persevering: steadfastness.[1]

Left for dead. Starving. Dehydrated. A long, long way from home. Even from dry land. Welcome to the life of Louis Zamperini in the summer of 1943.

Laura Hillenbrand's brilliant book, *Unbroken*, is the true story of this American Olympic and World War II hero. The book describes the remarkable courage and perseverance he showed throughout his life. Following the crash of his bomber plane over the Pacific Ocean in May of 1943, Zamperini had to fight to stay alive. This fight would continue for over two years. He was stranded at sea for 47 days on a raft and survived. Then, he became a prisoner of war in several

Japanese camps until the end of the war in August of 1945. He survived and won his freedom.

Zamperini was born into a family of Italian immigrants in Olean, New York, in 1917. The family later relocated to Torrance, California, just south of Los Angeles. From a very young age, Zamperini had to fight for everything he had. He and his brother were the targets of bullies, largely because they did not speak English. He grew up angry and defensive, getting in fights in his neighborhood and vigorously defending himself. He also grew up in a very competitive athletic environment which gave him the outlet he needed to shine. He became a track star and later ran in the 1936 Olympics in Berlin. He appeared destined to become a world champion. Instead, he chose to serve his country.

66 *To persevere is important to everybody. Don't give up, don't give in. There is always an answer to everything."— Louis Zamperini*

Louis Zamperini survived unfathomable conditions and barbaric torture during his days as a POW. He refused to give in to defeat. He had been a competitor and fighter his entire life. He had dreams of continuing his track career following the war. He wanted to build a life filled with competitive pursuits and family activities.

Zamperini fended off death at every turn. He was nearly eaten by sharks. Starvation and dehydration somehow evaded him. He survived life on the raft. He suffered dehumanization, humiliation, and mental and physical torture in the prisoner camps. Despite all this, Zamperini would not give up or surrender his will to anyone or anything.

The man's willpower was indestructible. Combined with his belief that he would survive, Zamperini showed the remarkable power of the human spirit. Even in the midst of unimaginable horrors he was able to persevere and make it out of the war alive.

The Core of Perseverance

" *We don't develop courage by being happy every day. We develop it by surviving difficult times and challenging adversity."—Barbara De Angelis*

Perseverance is the secret formula we use to our advantage that helps us power our way through any circumstance or predicament. It's a blessing filled with fortitude and unwavering determination that allows us to pursue whatever we desire. Perseverance gives life to all the values in this book. It unifies our belief in ourselves and others. Perseverance is believing that you are never, ever defeated because you will never, ever give up.

Think of how horrifying and frightening Louis Zamperini's circumstances must have been. He had just lost eight of his friends in a fatal plane crash. His whole world came crashing down and he didn't have any time to grieve. It was immediately time to survive. You may not have to fend off sharks, but sooner or later, you will need to overcome adversity. You may be dealing with an illness, a financial worry, or maybe you just lost your job. It takes resolve and the dynamic power of the human spirit to resist the urge to give in. This is where the value of perseverance helps us realize how much power we have inside us, and that we must carry on.

" *It's not how many times you get knocked down, it's whether you get back up." — Sylvester Stallone, Rocky*

Adversity and temporary failure come to define us. Perseverance gives us the fuel we need to advance toward achieving the next goal in front of us. When we are affected by setbacks, it's up to us to keep moving forward. Not out of revenge or anger, but out of desire, grit, determination and renewed enthusiasm. This is where "fire" comes from. We need to stoke and fan the fire inside of us with sensory imagery that makes us feel alive. We can stimulate our minds to produce positive energy and will ourselves toward action and positive outcomes.

Everyone fails at one point or another. Sometimes, the way we get knocked down is completely out of our control. But we must respond and rise to the occasion. Strong-minded and determined people will themselves into better circumstances through perseverance. This iron will begins with our attitude and effort. We move forward by relentlessly pursuing dreams, goals, and fulfillment of self. We must not settle for second-best.

" *Defeat is a state of mind; no one is ever defeated until defeat has been accepted as a reality." —Bruce Lee*

Think of perseverance as a safeguard—a hard-earned insurance policy against giving in to your worst fears. Perseverance allows you to think with greater energy. It opens you up to more opportunity and optimism. Perseverance keeps you thinking forward and being forward, while focusing on what's important each day. It keeps an eye on the design of future planning that is essential for attaining your goals. Perseverance enables you to live a life without regret. There is no life worth living that involves regret.

Obstacles to Living with Perseverance

- Doubt

- Fear

- Procrastination

- Lack of confidence

- Criticism and pressure

I find with each passing day the biggest critic in my life is the person I look at each morning in the mirror. This is both a blessing and a curse. I demand a lot of myself. I have enormous dreams that most people would probably laugh at and dismiss. Sometimes, in moments of weakness, I cave in to fears and temporary worries.

While inner doubt is real—and a battle worth fighting each day— I find that criticism also comes in many shapes and sizes. A snide comment. A dismissive retort to an idea at work. Even someone close to you casting aspersions over a speech you gave or song you played at a gig. You must survive criticism if you want to find happiness, success, and peace of mind. I've seen rising businesswomen, writers, comedians, lawyers, and athletes melt under the burning heat of criticism. It's sickening to watch, and it can be avoided. You have to persevere and carry on.

Are you your biggest critic? Do you keep your dreams to yourself or are you willing to share them with others?

The closer we get to achieving our dreams—which are a direct byproduct of living with purpose and adherence to our values—the more we encounter diversions or temptations. These are true "time-wasters" meant to distract and veer us off course. We all need motivating factors at the beginning of each day that we can read aloud and speak over our lives. So, I ask you, what can you conjure up in your beautiful imagination that will help influence your thoughts? What will inspire you to fight off your inner critic and the words of those who doubt you?

Once you have those, you can feed these emotions to your subconscious mind through the power of autosuggestion. Autosuggestion is, "an influencing of one's own attitudes, behavior, or physical condition by mental processes other than conscious thought."[2] Most people don't do this because it takes discipline, mindfulness, and rigor. It requires composure and extraordinary emotional intelligence. Some people are scared of what they might tell themselves. They're fearful of success or what might happen once they decide never to look back upon doubt, criticism, and fear.

As Robin Williams' character tells Matt Damon's in *Good Will Hunting*: "You're terrified of what you might say." Some of us don't believe we're worthy to speak such positive things over our lives. But this is what we must do if we want to defeat outer and inner criticism. Create this fertile ground in your mind before you take the action required.

After you have the thought process, mental preparation, and autosuggestion down, focus on these **five areas**:

1. Define your values and establish goals.

2. Design a weekly road map that can be refined, refreshed, and modified as need be. (This is an iterative, living plan. It should be reviewed multiple times per day.)

3. Envision yourself performing each goal and task in your plan.

4. Do the work: concentrate all your energy, effort, and attitude on each task.

5. Celebrate the small wins and large victories.

Value within the Value

A Story to Tell

I'm a big fan of John Mayer's music and his personal story. Like Mayer's path to success, my love of his music did not happen overnight. It came with time. It wasn't until I saw him perform live and listened to him speak about his personal journey that I began to develop a connection with him as an artist. Four years ago, on a magical night at Jones Beach on Long Island, his guitar-playing and words captivated my imagination in a way few musicians ever have.

Mayer spoke about his struggles starting out as a musician and how he managed to persevere through moments of doubt. As he went on, I had a powerful feeling come over me that, even to this day, is a bit hard to put into words. It felt so real and gripping. As I listened to his words, I started to think about my life. I thought about my dreams—you know, the ones I had started but had been too afraid to follow through on. I began to make sense of my past experiences. It was a beautiful, spiritual experience. For the rest of that show, I imagined all my dreams coming true. I made a promise to myself to keep learning and applying values like perseverance, dedication, and commitment to my daily endeavors. When I got home from the show that night, I wrote down the following words:

Life is about taking the dreams God plants into our hearts and minds and activating them with faith and desire to carry them out to the best of our ability.

These became words to live by for me.

Mayer was a guitar prodigy from the time he was a teenager. He attended the prestigious Berklee College of Music in Boston for one year. He later dropped out to pursue his musical dream in Atlanta. Mayer started on his way to fame by playing clubs and bars with only a few people in attendance. He spoke of how each night, with each show, he was hoping to build his audience by ten or fifteen more people. He wanted to keep playing in front of bigger crowds, one gig at a time. He knew it wouldn't happen right away, but he felt that perseverance and talent would form a winning combination.

Seven Grammy awards (including nineteen nominations) and several multi-platinum records later, it's safe to say Mayer has made it. If someone with genius-like talent such as John Mayer doesn't achieve success right away, take heart: it's okay if you aren't an overnight success story. Very few people are. Their examples only distort your vision of reality. They can do harm to your personal growth, confidence, and belief in yourself which are paramount to achieving your dreams. Patience, as the saying goes, is a virtue.

Don't Get Left Behind

What is your field of expertise? Whether you're a guitar god, software engineer, project manager, or student, you'd better be ready for a lifetime of continuous learning. A high school or college education simply doesn't cut it anymore. There are always advances and innovations in every profession. The world moves fast, change is swift, and new skills—even in the field that you know best—are essential. Technology has an influence on every profession. You must be willing to adapt, lest you get left behind.

For some perspective, twenty years ago some writers were still using typewriters. If you don't know what a typewriter is, remember: Google is your friend! It may sound crazy, but I still remember typing term papers during my early high school years on a typewriter. My family didn't get a personal computer until after I left home for college. (Hey, we weren't exactly the family of cutting-edge technology!)

The point is, writing became much different with the advent of computers, blogging and digital publishing. The ability to instantly get your message out to billions of people was a game-changer. This technology has also dramatically changed many other professions. Whether your thing is social media, broadcasting, carpentry, hair-cutting, or flying planes, if you want it badly enough, you'll build time into your schedule to learn. You may need to out of necessity. You may simply want to learn something new. Concentrate your energy on what drives and stirs positive emotions inside you. Then—*keep going*. I think you'll find life is much more rewarding when your intellectual curiosity leads you to places you never could have imagined.

A Story to Tell

> " *In every adversity there lies the seed of an equivalent advantage. In every defeat is a lesson showing you how to win the victory next time.*" —*Robert Collier*

"ADVERSITY!!!" I can still hear the booming yell of one of my fellow assistant coaches in the halftime locker room. My second year of coaching high school basketball took place at a public school in northern Virginia. It was one of the most inspiring learning experiences of my life. It's no exaggeration to say, I'm who I am today because for one season, I was in an environment rich in spirit and camaraderie.

Our lead assistant coach was the father of the head coach. This gave the team a family environment. It made it fun to observe father and son working in tandem as teachers to young men. One of my dreams has always been to coach a game with my father on the sidelines, so it was cool to live vicariously through our coaching staff. Our lead assistant provided me with the best framework I have for confronting and conquering life's perennial foe: adversity.

He used to stop practices and deliver his ringing yell— "ADVERSITY!"—during pivotal moments. He'd look into the eyes of our kids and then ask, "What are you gonna do?!" Coach knew during key moments, it was all about how our players—and we as a team— would respond. Would we fall apart? Would we dig deep and persevere? How we reacted would determine not just wins and losses, but our character and resolve.

We realized we needed a game plan that strengthened our preparation for adverse moments. During one of our biggest games of the season, we beat T.C. Williams High School—the school made famous by the movie, *Remember The Titans*, which starred Denzel Washington. This was the first time in seven seasons our school beat the Titans.

There's a reason, several years later, I still think of that game. In the past, our team would fade late in the game. It wasn't because of endurance or strength, but because we lacked the mental fortitude. The only way we'd overcome our biggest rival was by learning to persevere first in our minds. Our season-long journey gave us a courtside seat for watching our players overcome adversity. We worked each day toward putting together a complete performance. We preached perseverance to our players, and it came to fruition that game.

There's no avoiding adversity. We must face it head on and persevere. Chances are, you've faced considerable adversity in your life. How are you handling it? Do you run away and hope it will blow over? Or do you face it and resolve to change your circumstances? Inside all of us—at our core—is an indomitable will that desires to reach the zenith of our humanity. This is what psychologist Abraham Maslow dubbed "self-actualization."[3] When we exert ourselves to the maximum of attitude and effort, we find out who we really are. We'll find ourselves in these moments time and again in life. So, as my fellow coach used to say, "What are you gonna do?"

3 Questions on Perseverance to Ask Yourself:

1. Do you easily quit on things that you believe in?

2. Who in your life is an example or testament to perseverance? Reach out to that person to best understand what makes them tick.

3. What do you find is the biggest hurdle preventing you from continuing toward a goal or dream you believe in?

Results of Perseverance

Instant success is highly unlikely. In many ways, it would seem so unnatural because it would stunt growth—and life is all about growing and maturing. One of the battles we all face is the desire for instant gratification—for things to happen quickly and on our time. Reality begs to differ. Many of us are fortunate to receive what we ask for, but not on our time. I've grown to believe that life occurs on God's time, usually with some lessons learned and a heaping dose of humility, patience and perseverance.

The world is always challenging us to show patience. Sometimes, we are well equipped to handle the waiting or, even more difficult, the not-knowing. Other times, a lack of patience can affect our state of mind and handicap our lucid thinking. Impatience can lead to anxiety, which clouds our mind, causing us to worry and fear.

You'll experience thrills and enjoyment on the journey of instant gratification. But in the end, you won't get very far if you only think *what you want* will come *when you want it*. If you've ever followed a dream with all your heart, you already know the instant gratification world we live in is telling you a big lie. Talent and a tremendous work ethic will take you far in life. Patience, perseverance, and a resolute mindset will take you further.

I'll finish this chapter with a poem by Walter D. Wintle, which I first saw in Napoleon Hill's masterpiece, *Think and Grow Rich*. Any time I think I can't go on, I read this. I hope you reap the benefits of its wisdom, just as I have:

THINKING

If you think you are beaten, you are;

If you think you dare not, you don't.

If you'd like to win, but you think you can't,

It is almost a cinch that you won't.

If you think you'll lose, you're lost;

For out of the world we find

Success begins with a fellow's will

It's all in the state of mind.

If you think you're outclassed, you are;

You've got to think high to rise.

You've got to be sure of yourself before

You can ever win the prize.

Life's battles don't always go

To the stronger or faster man (or woman);

But sooner or later the man (or woman) who wins

Is the one who thinks he (she) can! [4]

Game Plan

1. Surround yourself with empowering visuals. Consider subscribing to a daily or weekly newsletter (such as mine!

chrisdconnors.com) that offers positive thoughts and encouragement. Spend time writing your thoughts each day. Focus on your pain points—the things that agitate you and serve as road blocks that prevent you from being happy. Identify these things, then determine a plan for how to overcome them. Concentrate on positive thinking, activity, and willpower.

2. Perseverance is a "repeatable process" mindset. It's a state of mind that you bring into each day, practice, class, game, meeting, exam, or creative venture. Burn this mindset into your memory and fuse it with things that motivate you. I like to think of my family, living my dreams and celebrating my successes. Visualize what you love. See the end-goal. Go for it!

Notes

[1] "Perseverance," *Merriam-Webster*,
https://www.merriam-webster.com/dictionary/perseverance (accessed May 31, 2017).

[2] "Autosuggestion," *Merriam-Webster*,
https://www.merriam-webster.com/dictionary/autosuggestion (accessed May 31, 2017)

[3] Abraham H. Maslow, Motivation and Personality. 2nd ed., Chapter 11 "Self-Actualizing People: A Study of Psychological Health"

[4] Napoleon Hill, *Think and Grow Rich* (Robbinsdale, MN: Fawcett Publications, 1937) via 1905 – Unity. Published in 1905 by Unity Tract Society, Unity School of Christianity

V
Mindfulness

CHAPTER 18

Positive Attitude (Optimism)

"When you truly have a positive attitude, you capture that energy of what can be accomplished, as opposed to why it can't be done... I ask you to thoroughly examine your attitude, to make it positive and to go forth and make your mark on this world." [1]

— *Cal Ripken Jr., Commencement Address at the University of Maryland, 2013*

DEFINITION:

Attitude: (a) a mental position with regard to a fact or state (b) a feeling or emotion toward a fact or state [2]

Optimism: an inclination to put the most favorable construction upon actions and events or to anticipate the best possible outcome [3]

Cancer.

One of the most frightening words in the English language. You may know someone whose life has been affected by cancer. It will turn a person's life upside down and at its worst, it's fatal. Yet there are stories—miracles—of those who were given the grace and good fortune to persevere and overcome this terrible disease. James

Conner, now a NFL football player, is one of them. It is within his story that we find the secret of inspiration that applies to us all.

After a thrilling stomp through the 2014 college football season, James Conner was named a First-Team All American and ACC conference player of the year. He entered the 2015 football season for the University of Pittsburgh ready to break records and dash his way to the NFL. Fate had a change of plans. On the first game of the season, he tore his MCL. He had to sit the entire season.

This was a tough blow—one that would be worst-case scenario for most athletes. However, the toughest news was yet to come. Right before Thanksgiving in 2015, Conner found out that he was diagnosed with Hodgkins lymphoma—a form of cancer. Would he ever play football again? More importantly, would he survive?

Now what?

❝*Once you go through something like this of this magnitude, no other human, really, I believe can stop me. That's the edge I have."*
– James Conner

It would take 12 rounds of chemotherapy just to try beating cancer. Each round of chemo is a grueling ordeal for any person to have to deal with. Even before it begins, there is the mental, emotional and physical preparation. A person has to be willing to commit to overcoming such a formidable foe. With each passing day, Conner kept powering through.

His teammates marveled at his ability to go for chemotherapy, then work out just as vigorously as them—and with them! He was a member of the University of Pittsburgh football team and he would fulfill his obligation to the team. He didn't want anyone to feel sorry for him. He wanted to set an example, as the captain of his team, that he would be a leader through anything.

Miraculously, six months later, after his twelfth—and final—chemotherapy treatment, Conner's cancer was gone. The treatment had worked. But in his view, the power to fight cancer began in his mind. His secret weapon? A positive attitude.

"...amazing willpower to go along with an "I'm not gonna be denied" mentality... those are two things I bring to the table every time I suit up." [4]

Conner's story highlights one man's fight against a deadly disease, and the indomitable power of the human spirit. He's a survivor and an example that we can truly overcome anything. His story is the perfect tale of inspiration. Even when our chips seem down, we're never out. We'll face countless challenges in life, some bigger than others. How we respond is often a function of what motivates us internally. We're motivated by what inspires us. We're inspired by our ability to stay positive and have faith.

The secret of inspiration is to look within at the boldness of your human spirit. All us of have something intangible, something magical inside of us that inspires and lights the way. Everything great in your life will first come from within. Believe in yourself and stay positive. You'll break records and beat impossible odds.

The Core of a Positive Attitude

Let's be real—we crave control. There is an empowering feeling that comes from knowing we are the ones calling the shots, kind of like we're Bill Gates. As the quote at the beginning of this chapter shows, we are always in control of our attitude. Given that we are, it would make sense that we live with a positive attitude, so that all areas of our lives are in harmony. Shawn Achor, the *New York Times* bestselling author of *The Happiness Advantage*, focuses on the powers that are unleashed when we live with a positive attitude: "Research shows that when people work with a positive mindset, performance on nearly every level—productivity, creativity, engagement—improves."[5]

Productivity. Creativity. Engagement. Look at those words again. Who of us doesn't want to live in the moment and find greater success? In addition to serving as a mindset, a positive attitude trains our brain and allows us to "rewire" the way we think through new habits and thoughts. Achor writes: "Training your brain to be positive is not so different from training your muscles at the gym. Recent research on neuroplasticity—the ability of the brain to change even in adulthood—reveals that as you develop new habits, you rewire the brain."[6]

So much for habits being unbreakable. You *can* teach an old dog new tricks! Our willpower and attitude are strong enough to help us change course, no matter our age. We all struggle with varying degrees of stubbornness. Think about it—you can end any kind of stubbornness at any time. We may not want to take out the garbage or fold the laundry, but the only thing getting in the way is our attitude. Trust me, your spouse or partner will thank you for it! Attitude is a choice within our control.

We don't need scientific data or research to persuade us of the benefits of a positive attitude, but rather to reaffirm our beliefs. Living with a positive attitude is something we likely already know. It's the matter of being positive each day that can be difficult. Life gets in the way. There's work, co-workers, bills and traffic jams. There's that "weekend" assignment that comes in our inbox at 4:57 on a Friday afternoon, right when we're about to get the party started. D'oh! These things can sometimes suck the life out of us. This is why the core of having a positive attitude means keeping our focus on the big picture, as well as the fine details. We need a long-term view, so we don't get bogged down by the small, sometimes frustrating, things.

Attitude and Effort Quadrant

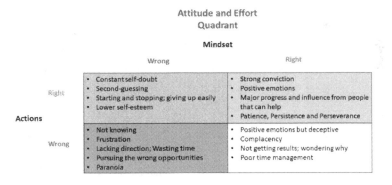

As you see in the quadrant, the optimal state is to have a positive, believing mindset backed with constructive actions. Here, we have strong faith, confidence, and receptiveness to new opportunities. We're willing to be patient and persevere because we believe in what we're doing. What's most damaging is to do the wrong thing and have a poor attitude. But I've found that doing the right thing, while believing what we're doing has been in vain, can lead to low self-esteem and worry.

Attitude adjustments can be corrected, or re-wired as Shawn Achor writes, over time. Changing our attitude is a matter of willpower. This requires breaking down old habits that have discouraged and held us back from our potential. Our goal should be to move to the upper-right part of the quadrant, where our actions are in line with a right mindset. Strong conviction doesn't equal stubbornness. Strong conviction and belief in yourself equals faith. This leads to perseverance. You'll never be able to get by with only a positive attitude, but it is crucial that you have this first.

In this life, we can only concern ourselves with deep focus and intent on the things we can control. Worrying will not add a single hour to our lives. In fact, it can and will rob us of our joy. It will take away time in peace, where we are in a happy emotional state. A negative attitude is destructive. Let's surround ourselves with positive people and environments. This is the first step toward a fulfilling and happy social life.

Obstacles to Living with a Positive Attitude

"As a single footstep will not make a path on the earth, so a single thought will not make a pathway in the mind. To make a deep physical path, we walk again and again. To make a deep mental path, we must think over and over the kind of thoughts we wish to dominate our lives." — Henry David Thoreau

- Negative attitude

- Worry

- Despair for the future

- Lack of self-awareness

We have to remind ourselves we're better than whatever anger, worry, doubt, or envy creeps into our minds. The surefire way to block these thoughts out is to dominate our subconscious minds with positive thoughts, rooted in belief of self. Our values, self-confidence, and things that matter help give us that view. With this in mind, I urge you to try something very simple: Dedicate time throughout your day to speak positive, affirming words over your life. Set a reminder on your smartphone or in your daily journal. Every thirty minutes, speak positive words over your life. It makes an enormous difference.

When I find myself in moments where I feel like I'm stuck or anxious and my mind starts drifting, I think of my beautiful family. I smile as I envision my son developing into a star athlete. I focus on my dreams—the things that light the fire inside of me. These thoughts inspire me to keep moving forward with confidence, energy, and hope every day. I think of my *Why*—my definition of success—and my passion for writing, coaching, and helping others. Those things lift my spirit and produce tidal waves of positive energy inside of me.

What are those things for you? Remember—these should be simple things.

We all experience the proverbial peaks and valleys for a reason. The down periods help us to put things in perspective and make better sense of the highs. We should never remain down for too long, because this leads to worry. Worrying never helps, yet we're human, so we turn to worry. *Worry about our life, worry about our parents or friends, worry about what others think of our latest Instagram post.* Think about it—when has that ever helped you? Part of living with a positive attitude is accepting life as it comes, while having an expectation that good things will happen.

Value within the Value

66*It's not what we do once in a while that shapes our lives. It's what we do consistently."—Tony Robbins*

Accomplishments and awards stand out to us, but the people we admire most are those who work hard and have a positive attitude. I marvel at single mothers who care for their children and work several jobs to make ends meet. I'm inspired by business professionals who work high-pressure jobs, and still find time to volunteer for charities.

I encourage you to adopt an "abundance mindset," one with a *being* belief where you already *have* the objects of your desire. This creates a positive attitude of expectancy. I acknowledge that this isn't easy to cultivate when we're doing something or performing the tasks of a job that we don't love. This is why I'm an enormous proponent of finding enthusiasm and fire for *something* in your life. I encourage you to dedicate at least part of your day to immersing yourself in that. Are you doing this now?

This takes consistency and planning. We perform our best work and become who we're destined to be by spending time doing what we love. This may not come in the form of a job. It may come from spending time with our family or friends. It may come from coaching youth baseball, volunteering at the local library, or going mountain biking. It may come from jamming out some monster guitar solos in our room when no one's looking. Activities that get us excited help put us in a good mood, which helps us have a positive outlook on life. It's how we integrate these with consistency that makes a big difference in our happiness.

A Story to Tell

A few days before the start of my college basketball career, my high school coach mailed me a greeting card with an inspiring message. It was one of those "positive thinking" cards. You know, the kind you've likely seen at doctors' offices or on your boss's office wall:

ATTITUDE

Attitude Is A Little Thing That Makes A BIG Difference

In fact, this is the *exact* cover of the card. The card's exterior was not what inspired me. Rather, it was the words inside that proved to be most valuable. I was a good high school player, and I earned a scholarship to play basketball at the college level. I was also a hothead, at times. I didn't do a great job of controlling my emotions on the court. My high school coach knew that. He knew I had the talent and drive to succeed as a college player. The purpose of his card was to remind me of one essential point, which he wrote inside: *"You have the talent to play at this level. It's your attitude that will make the difference of whether you're successful or not."*

What he meant was, I had all the tools to be a successful player. I'd go as far as my ability to control my emotions. While I didn't previously think of things this way, I came to realize my attitude was equally as important as my effort. I kept those words in mind as I navigated my first year of college basketball. I improved as a player, and received a first-class education in emotional maturity and the importance of a positive attitude. I've taken that lesson with me throughout my life.

We're all going to face adverse, new circumstances throughout our lives. The key is to keep moving forward, embrace change, and maintain a positive attitude. You can't always control the outcomes, but you can control your attitude. How you harness your attitude will determine how well you compete on the playing field of life. Your attitude will determine whether exciting opportunities and new relationships come your way. No matter where you are currently, I'm willing to bet you have the tools you need to be happy and successful. Realize your attitude will guide your direction.

Results of a Positive Attitude

As I put forward in Chapter 3 on Hope, I encourage you to develop an inspirational routine each morning. It may come through the power of meditation, prayer, music, or conversation with people you love. It could be a video that plays back the piano recital you played to perfection that brought the house down. It may be the words of a passage in a book or a voicemail from a dear friend— words you hold in such high esteem, you get the chills before reading or listening. Develop your routine; it will place you in a positive frame of mind.

There's plenty of science that shows a positive attitude will help you relieve stress and become healthier. Here are some of the benefits of positive thinking, per the Mayo Clinic:

- Increased life span

- Lower rates of depression

- Lower levels of distress

- Greater resistance to the common cold

- Better psychological and physical well-being

- Better cardiovascular health and reduced risk of death from cardiovascular disease

- Better coping skills during hardships and times of stress [7]

Eric Kim, a research fellow at Harvard University's Department of Social and Behavioral Sciences, and his fellow researchers found even more science behind the net effects of positive health in a recent study. Kim says, "We should make efforts to boost optimism, which has been shown to be associated with healthier behaviors and healthier ways of coping with life challenges." [8] Further, the study adds:

"Growing evidence has linked positive psychological attributes like optimism to a lower risk of poor health outcomes, especially cardiovascular disease. It has been demonstrated in randomized trials that optimism can be learned." [9]

We're successful when we surround ourselves with people and things that create positive energy. The thoughts that enter our minds can change both our emotional and physical states. Norman Vincent Peale addressed this beautifully in his book, *The Power of Positive Thinking*: "We are beginning to comprehend a basic truth hitherto neglected, that our physical condition is determined very largely by our emotional condition, and our emotional life is profoundly regulated by our thought life." [10]

Given all the reward for thinking positively, why would we ever want to turn to the negative?

Game Plan

1. Every time you approach a new opportunity, approach it with an "I will do this" attitude. Master control over your thoughts to reject any possibility of failure. If you believe and will yourself into thinking you can do something, you will find a way.

2. Your attitude can be influenced by tapping into the power of your subconscious mind, which serves as a data repository and recordkeeper of all your thoughts. Keep feeding your

mind positive thoughts. Constantly work your analytical mind to diagram plans for success. This takes vision! Your vision is best achieved by preparing your mind to think positively. Live with a winning mindset—one where you program your mind toward success. This will continue to build up your spirit, self-confidence, and faith. As you build yourself up, you'll find an increase in your adrenaline, which is the fuel that will drive you further than you ever thought possible.

Notes

[1] "Cal Ripken Jr. Inspires Graduates to Keep a Positive Attitude," University of Maryland Alumni Association, http://umd.imodules.com/s/1132/form2016.aspx?sid=1132&gid=1&pgid=2172 (accessed May 31, 2017).

[2] "Attitude," *Merriam-Webster*, https://www.merriam-webster.com/dictionary/attitude (accessed May 31, 2017).

[3] "Optimism," *Merriam-Webster*, https://www.merriam-webster.com/dictionary/optimism (accessed May 31, 2017).

[4] "A Letter to NFL GMs," *The Player's Tribune* https://www.theplayerstribune.com/james-conner-pitt-letter-to-nfl-gms/ written by James Conner (accessed July 18, 2017)

[5] Shawn Achor, "Positive Intelligence," *Harvard Business Review*, January-February 2012, https://hbr.org/2012/01/positive-intelligence (accessed May 31, 2017).

[6] Ibid.

[7] "Positive thinking: Stop negative self-talk to reduce stress," Healthy lifestyle: Stress Management, Mayo Clinic, http://www.mayoclinic.org/healthy-lifestyle/stress-management/in-depth/positive-thinking/art-20043950 (accessed May 31, 2017).

[8] Eric Kim, quoted in Karen Feldscher, "How power of positive thinking works," *Harvard Gazette*, December 7, 2016, http://news.harvard.edu/gazette/story/2016/12/optistic-women-live-longer-are-healthier/ (accessed May 31, 2017).

[9] Eric S. Kim, Kaitlin A. Hagan, Francine Grodstein, et al., "Optimism and Cause-Specific Mortality: A Prospective Cohort Study," *American Journal of Epidemiology*, January 4, 2017, https://academic.oup.com/aje/article-abstract/185/1/21/2631298/Optimism-and-Cause-Specific-Mortality-A?sid=7816bd15-60fd-491b-bd99-f2cd39646d10 (accessed May 31, 2017).

[10] Dr. Norman Vincent Peale, *The Power of Positive Thinking: A Practical Guide to Mastering the Problems of Everyday Living* (NJ: Prentice-Hall, 1952).

CHAPTER 19

Open-Mindedness

*"Open your eyes to the beauty around you, open your mind
to the wonders of life, open your heart to those who love you,
and always be true to yourself."*

—*Donna Davis*

DEFINITION:

Receptive to arguments or ideas.[1]

*Open Mind: a willingness to listen to or accept different ideas or
opinions* [2]

Sixteen million records! Any band, in any genre, could only hope
that a miracle might deliver that much success over the course of a
fifty-year career. Yet that is the tally (and still counting) for Hootie
and The Blowfish's debut album, *Cracked Rear View*. Darius Rucker,
known as "Hootie," is the primary songwriter and mastermind
behind the group's success. He helped elevate the band to the top of
the music charts in the mid 1990's. As the decade wore on, the band
enjoyed two more successful albums, both of which went platinum.
But gradually, the group fell out of favor with the public. The times

were a changin' and like any artists, Hootie and the boys would need to reinvent themselves.

For Darius Rucker, living with an open mind is a way of life. He's done it in his personal and professional relationships, as well as his career opportunities. Rucker started Hootie and the Blowfish with his college buddies in 1986, while attending the University of South Carolina. He was a black man (with white bandmates) in a mostly white alternative music scene. He encountered racism and resistance.[3] But he kept doing what he loved and didn't worry about what a few haters had to say. Rucker wouldn't let his skin color define him. He kept an open mind and let his musical talents do the talking.

He later made the transition to a completely different genre of music: country. It was a smooth and highly successful one.[4] His debut country album went platinum. He's turned out two more gold albums. Despite achieving so much, Rucker didn't ask for any big breaks or handouts.

"I said to my label when we went in, 'I want to do everything the new guy does.' I went to 120 radio stations—I mean, five days a week, four or five stations a day." [5]

He knew a tireless work ethic and a mind open to new opportunity would lead him to success in a new venture. After all, it took seven long years before Hootie and the Blowfish hit mainstream success with their debut album. Very rarely does success happen overnight. Rucker's life is testament to the importance of open-mindedness in relationships and opportunities. He's managed two different careers, both with wild success. He figured out how to form rewarding friendships and business relationships. He refused to let discrimination hold him back from living the life he wanted. The secret? A willingness to keep an open mind.

The Core of Open-Mindedness

The great Walt Disney once said, "If you can dream it, you can do it." These are words my mom and dad have said to me throughout my life. Maybe you've heard them from your parents and teachers. Open-mindedness promotes curiosity, while urging us to welcome change and new opinions. There is greater freedom of mind that comes from living an open-minded life. Open-mindedness makes us receptive to new ideas and gives us an attitude of acceptance. This adds peace and harmony to our lives.

An open-minded person lives this mantra: "Every adversity presents an opportunity of an equivalent advantage."[6] The open-minded person can accept temporary difficulty and turn it into a triumph. Open-mindedness is built on trust, faith, and acceptance of a call to action in our lives. It is the antithesis, or direct opposite, of intolerance. It means we're fair-minded and willing to entertain new thoughts and ideas, and open to meeting new people.

Open-mindedness is not only about tolerance, though that is a large part of it. It's an act of willpower that requires courage. It implies that we are open to change, which is the evolution of our thought and maturity as humans and thinkers. When we evolve and improve upon our knowledge, we gain greater wisdom and clarity. We become more likely to grow, and hungrier to learn and expand our minds. In business and in our personal lives, open-mindedness and curiosity are equally important.

How important is open-mindedness, not just to you, but in the view of leaders in business? According to a 2015 PwC survey of more than one-thousand CEOs, many cited "curiosity" and "open-mindedness" as leadership traits that are becoming increasingly critical in challenging times.[7]

There's a reason for this: companies need employees to think creatively, solve problems and identify solutions. If you're curious and open-minded, you're much more valuable to your employer. This same logic carries over to what you desire in life. To live a fulfilling life on your terms, you need creative ideas. To get the ideas, you need to have an open mind receptive to new information. Then, you back those ideas with faith, discipline, and hard work.

A great way to embrace curiosities is to plan them into your week. You can learn a new language by using the plethora of online resources at your disposal. But before you do, set aside thirty minutes on your calendar and dedicate the time. Curiosities lead to open-mindedness, and they only elude us when we think we don't have the time. Keep finding activities that stimulate creative, imaginative thought. Make the time for them. These add value to you as an individual—both in the way others see you and in how you see yourself. We all have things we love that are tried and true. But what about trying new things?

It's amazing the new ideas we'll find—and remarkable, new experiences we'll enjoy—when we're open-minded and willing to give it a shot.

Obstacles to Living with Open-Mindedness

- Prejudices, biases, and stereotypes

- Close-mindedness: unwillingness to give things a chance

- Rejecting opportunity

- Negative thoughts

How often do you judge someone you've never even met? Think about people in your work or school life that you don't really know. How many of these people have you formed a strong opinion about? In some instances, you may not even know more than their first name. There's a lot of black and white polarization in our culture—though not just based on the color of our skin. Too often, we take absolute points of view that we're unwilling to compromise on before we have the facts. This ends up being counterproductive in several ways, but none more so than closing ourselves off to an opposing point of view. This is the definition of being close-minded.

Close-mindedness decreases our capacity and desire to understand—to learn! We form stereotypes and cynical views, thinking of other people's beliefs as dangerous. This way of thinking creates anger, negativity, and a poor attitude. It leads us away from positive emotions, creative thoughts, and new ideas. You've probably been there before, getting worked up over unimportant things that can destroy your day or even your week.

You have a huge presentation at 3pm, then you have to pick up the kids from daycare, but you're at odds with your husband over ne political protest that's been in the news. All of a sudden, your emotions have gotten the better of you. You're worked up and off your game. Negativity and anxiety start to creep in. You fight to regain control.

We all encounter negative thoughts, which distract and frustrate us. These enemies keep us from living an open-minded life. They also prevent us from focusing on what author Dr. Stephen Covey called "quality time" in his famous time management matrix. Covey describes using new activities and methods to boost our personal growth as "sharpening the saw" time. This is where we learn, read, imagine new ideas, explore our creative side, and spend time in prayer. This is time we can build in—for at least five hours per week—to develop our minds.

Despite a busy schedule and juggling lots of responsibilities, we all have the time. We simply need to make it happen. Your future self will thank you for this time of development and enrichment.

Value within the Value

66 *The secret of change is to focus all of your energy, not on fighting the old, but on building the new."[8] —Dan Millman*

To live with an open mind means we embrace change and understand that the world around us, and our thoughts, will continue to evolve. Just as our positive values (like the ones in this book!) should remain constant, change is a constant of life. Change is simply going to keep coming at us. Either we create change or it happens to us. So, why do so many of us fight change? Why don't we concentrate and place our energy in "building the new" frontiers t. come with change, as the above quote suggests?

Very simply: change is hard.

Change will hit us throughout life, beginning right after high school. Whether we go to college or start a job, we must look to further ourselves. Once we get a job, we decide whether we'll stay there long-term or try something new. Chances are, this cycle will repeat itself a few more times throughout our careers. Change will challenge us and, at times, confuse us.

But change is also how we make sense of our world. Living with a mind receptive to new ideas and possibilities is not easy, though we must be open to it if we are to find ourselves. This is not to suggest that staying right where we are or holding our ground is always wrong. It's not. It depends on the circumstances and information at-hand. Life demands that we live with situational awareness, a creative imagination, and an analytical mind.

Situational awareness helps us prepare, react, and decide upon the various choices we need to make. An example of this is being able to identify when you're in a dead-end job or a position with an opportunity to grow. Creative imagination helps us think boldly and beautifully. This is where we form new ideas, like the idea for a book or how to paint the fine details of one of our favorite scenes in nature. An analytical mind acts as the processing station for the intake of information. This enables us to make smart decisions. We may want to take that trip to Paris, but we don't have the money saved up. Our analytical mind crunches the cost, time, and enjoyment factors, leading us toward our decision.

We all know people who have lived their whole life in the same town, or worked for the same employer their whole career. As long as they're happy and fulfilled, then that's all good. But change is not just about where we live or work. *Change is life.* Change is a mantra and mindset for how we prepare our minds to think clearly about all our decisions.

Think about it—would you change the way you make decisions if you knew you'd find better results by living with a mindset open to change? I'm willing to bet you would. Yet too many of us have myopic ways of thinking and only focus on short-term gains. Here's the problem with that: When we don't have a long-term strategy or plan, we lack the proper perspective. We need to see our lives from a high-level view, not just the ground-level. In the short-term, it's easy to think only about trudging forward. We then fail to question why or to think in a strategic way. Everything becomes tactical.

So, when we inevitably make a "wrong turn" or need to change direction, it's so much harder because we lack the big-picture perspective. It becomes harder to identify why things went wrong. We need to know why things went wrong, so we can game plan on how to make them right. Short-term thinking and strategy is always imperative. But if it's not accompanied by a big-picture view that can recognize change, we're in trouble.

Life is going to change many, many more times. You must be willing to approach it with a positive attitude and open mind. Look back with fondness at the people and things that came before, but keep powering into the future with confidence and enthusiasm. Life is full of rewards for those who live boldly. The secret of change is to keep going.

Keep Going

> " *If someone is able to show me that what I think or do is not right, I will happily change, for I seek the truth, by which no one was ever truly harmed. It is the person who continues in his self-deception and ignorance who is harmed."—Marcus Aurelius*

We can always ward off cynicism and a "know-it-all" attitude by keeping an open mind and giving every matter the attention of a fresh, new look. Once we've suffered, been wronged, let down, dismissed, or hurt, it's harder for us to keep an open mindset of renewal. This is when we need to strengthen our willpower to believe and carry out any plans that we commit to action. We will encounter adversity and self-doubt, but we must persevere. Self-doubt and fear cause us to worry about the future. If we dwell too much on the future and what we don't have now, we lose sight of what is most important—living in the moment. By focusing only on what we haven't yet accomplished, or what we don't have in our lives, we lose sight of the task at hand. As Bono would tell you: "What you don't have, you don't need it now." A future-looking mindset is good, but only if it doesn't consume our present.

We'll find new opportunities and friendships, simply by entertaining new possibilities. To live a life of happiness and self-fulfillment, we must persevere and keep an open mind. When we are complacent, we settle. Then, negative emotions permeate our thoughts and affect how we see our path ahead. Imagination, curiosity, and optimism are driving forces of the emotionally intelligent mind. They are key components to living an open-minded life.

sults of Open-Mindedness

> ❝ *Hard work and an open mind—it's the only way to realize the potential that is inside every one of us."* [9] — *Chrissie Wellington*

It always begins with an idea. The fertile ground for the generation of ideas is a clear, open mind. Every authentic person I've met is someone who's open to new ideas. They may live by a code of values and morals that remain constant, but when it comes to opinions, people, and events, they're always open to listening. Authenticity asks that we judge free of bias and remain impartial in all affairs. Authentic people, I've found, are always open-minded and full of great ideas. They want to keep learning, growing, and educating their minds to further themselves.

I think of our education system. Some of us will graduate high school, go to college, and perhaps even advance to higher degrees. Regardless of the level that we climb, we may think our education culminates in the system. Then we can rest on our laurels and coast afterwards. Wrong! Life is all about continuing education. We have to keep learning, building relationships and challenging our minds.

I've had more opportunities come to me through being open-minded than from any other trait. I've coached CEOs of major companies, not because of my talents, but because I was open-minded and understanding of their needs. I showed that I cared. I wouldn't let any biases or prejudices cloud my mind.

My brother (as I discussed in the chapter on Hope) is a sports anchor at ESPN. Before he got to ESPN, he worked for CBS. The way he got there was by accepting an assignment on radio. He had never worked one professional day on radio, so he had his doubts. A talking things through with him, we both felt it would still be a goc move. He gave it a shot. He kept an open mind, and that radic opportunity soon led to a great TV opportunity with CBS. This exposure helped him land the job at ESPN.

The choice is yours. Live an open-minded life, full of exciting opportunities, or close yourself off and reduce your chances of living the life you truly desire. I hope you'll keep an open mind.

Game Plan

1. Create a curiosities list. This is a list of things that intrigue you, but which you know little about. This could be learning how to create your own website. Maybe it's trying out for a part in a play. Maybe it's learning about Artificial Intelligence (AI). Begin brainstorming on one curiosity per week. Jot down all the thoughts and ideas that come to mind. Keep pursuing it and watch as you add a fun, new hobby to your life.

2. Introduce yourself to one new person this week. It could be a friend at school or a work colleague you've been wanting to say, "Hi" to, but have never gotten around to connecting with. Maybe it's even a blind date! Be open to another person's ideas. Listen to what they have to say, even if at first you don't agree. You might learn something. Better yet, you might gain a new friend in the process.

Notes

1 "Open-minded," *Merriam-Webster*, https://www.merriam-webster.com/dictionary/open-mindedness (accessed May 30, 2017).

2 "Open-mind," *Merriam-Webster*, https://www.merriam-webster.com/dictionary/open-mind (accessed May 30, 2017).

3 Brian Mansfield, "Darius Rucker calls racist tweeter an 'idiot,'" *USA Today*, May 23, 2013, https://www.usatoday.com/story/life/2013/05/23/darius-rucker-racist-tweet-idiot/2352439/ (accessed May 30, 2017).

4 Brian Reynolds, "Changing his tune: Rucker's rise from former pop star to big-time country star," *Evansville Courier & Press*, February 1, 2010, http://archive.courierpress.com/features/changing-his-tune-ruckers-rise-from-former-pop-star-to-big-time-country-star-ep-446925347-324696691.html?bppw=absolutely&suppressAds=youbet (accessed May 30, 2017).

5 Darius Rucker, quoted in Will Hermes, "Darius Rucker: The Rock Transplants," *Rolling Stone*, June 19, 2014, http://www.rollingstone.com/music/features/the-rock-transplants-20140619 (accessed May 30, 2017).

6 Robert Collier quote; Goodreads, https://www.goodreads.com/author/quotes/257221.Robert_Collier (accessed May 24, 2017)

7 "20 years inside the mind of the CEO ... What's next?" PWC Global, http://www.pwc.com/gx/en/ceo-agenda/ceosurvey/2017/us (accessed May 30, 2017); and Warren Berger, "Why Curious People Are Destined for the C-Suite," *Harvard Business Review*, September 11, 2015, https://hbr.org/2015/09/why-curious-people-are-destined-for-the-c-suite (accessed May 30, 2017).

8 Dan Millman, *Way of the Peaceful Warrior: A Book that Changes Lives* (Tiburon, CA: HJ Kramer, Inc, 1984), 113.

9 Chrissie Wellington, *A Life without Limits: A Word Champion's Journey* (Center Street, 2012).

CHAPTER 20

Humility

"True humility is not thinking less of yourself; it is thinking of yourself less."

— C.S. Lewis

DEFINITION:

Humility: freedom from pride or arrogance [1]

Humble: (1) not proud or haughty (2) reflecting, expressing or offered in a spirit of deference or submission [2]

What makes someone a hero? Is it words? Actions? As Welles Crowther demonstrated in the chapter on Altruism, what defines women and men of great courage and integrity is their willingness to act in the service of others, with little concern for their own importance. The people who talk, act, and promote themselves—focusing only on themselves—tend to garner the most attention. That's an observation from the reality show society we live in.

But sometimes, heroes stand out because of their modesty and humility. The bold story of leadership and grace under pressure demonstrated by Captain Chesley Sullenberger—known universally as "Sully"— is testament to that.

ιortly after takeoff on the morning of January 15, 2009, US
ways Flight 1549 ran into some turbulence. The plane hit a large
ock of Canadian geese that destroyed both engines. Suddenly, a
routine flight from New York to Charlotte was in crisis mode, and
there was little time to act. The captain needed to diagnose the issue
and make a swift decision: Could he keep going? If this was an
emergency, would it even be possible to make an emergency landing
at a local airport?

Captain Sullenberger, a veteran of the skies and U.S. Air Force
captain, analyzed this precarious situation to the best of his ability.
He deemed the only possibility for survival was to try to land the
plane on water—in this case, the icy cold Hudson River, the narrow
waterway that flanks Manhattan Island's western shore.

Captain Sullenberger remained calm and poised. His only concern
was for the crew and passengers on board. Minutes later, he
successfully landed the plane, in extraordinarily difficult conditions,
in the middle of the river. After communicating with Air Traffic
Control, he helped facilitate the evacuation of all passengers on
board via rafts and the wings of the plane.

Everyone survived.

A hero was born, though admittedly, a reluctant one. That
moment catapulted the long-time airline pilot into the hearts of
many, leading to fame and recognition. As the adulation and showers
of praise began to flood in from media, passengers, New Yorkers, and
other Americans, Captain Sullenberger wasn't looking for attention.
He could have taken the moment to make it all about him. Instead,
he deflected the attention away from himself and thanked everyone

involved. He praised the team that made everything possible. I.
a defining display of humility by a man who has always put
country and fellow citizens before himself.

The 2016 movie *Sully* dramatically captures the events of that day,
and the surrounding National Transportation Safety Board (NTSB)
investigation into the crash. Tom Hanks, who plays Captain
Sullenberger, artfully delivered Sully's thoughts on the matter: "It
wasn't just me, it was all of us. Jeff, Donna, Shila and Dureene. And
all passengers, rescue workers. And traffic control, helicopter crews
and scuba cops. We all did it! We survived."

A humble hero, indeed.

The Core of Humility

> *It's what you learn after you know it all that counts."* —Coach John
> *Wooden*

The above words—from one of my leadership and coaching
heroes—are a great humility check. At least once a week, I look back
at this maxim and think about how much further I need to go to
become the man I desire to be. Despite how much I've learned, I
recognize how much I don't know. Part of being human is thinking
we know more than we really do. The truth is, we'll never, ever know
it all. Once we accept this, we open ourselves up to learning and
growing with greater passion and energy. Confidence matters a great
deal. Still, there must be an even-keel approach to life, a balance
between confidence and humility, to ensure arrogance and
complacency do not settle in.

e should be proud of what we accomplish. We should never e for granted any "wins" we earn, no matter how small or large. nis is the difference between a humble person and an arrogant one: a humble person accepts victories and praise, uses them for motivation, and continues moving forward by using their talents to benefit others. An arrogant person is more prone to selfishness. They take praise, often without gratitude, then continue to focus on their pursuits and "riches."

Humility leads us toward a transfer of mindset, from self-centered concern, to actions that are always fueled by virtuous, benevolent thoughts. I urge you to make one simple question the foundation and beginning of the words you wish to communicate to anyone you meet:

"How can I help you?"

I've found good fortune comes when you ask how you can help someone else. I think about my marriage each day. I get to share each day with the love of my life. The times when our relationship suffers are when I choose to act selfishly and put myself first. Our marriage fires on all cylinders when we both act with humility and kindness toward each other. We're at our best when we're actively invested in making each other's day brighter. It all starts with that question— "How can I help you?"

The favor is then returned without asking. And the spirit of our love becomes more powerful and bolder in magnitude. The power of love in our relationship is reciprocal—it's the giving of ourselves to one another that will last a lifetime.

" When we give cheerfully and accept gratefully, everyone blessed."—Maya Angelou

What if you chose today as the day to live out the Golden Rule and do unto others as you would like done for yourself? This is a principle, often attributed to the teachings of Jesus Christ. However, the Golden Rule actually predates Jesus. It is several thousands of years old. It has stood the test of time, because it appeals to our better human nature and brings joy, not just for one person but, for many.

Its value is exponentially greater when acted upon and shared with others!

" We only have what we give."—Isabel Allende

Demonstrate your passionate value in service to another person. It's the surest sign that the favor will be returned to you, perhaps in even greater abundance. Give without expecting anything in return. When you unleash the power of that mindset upon your everyday actions, you find a verve and enthusiasm that you didn't know previously existed. You stop thinking selfishly and start to act selflessly.

Obstacles to Living with Humility

- Boastfulness

- Pride and ego

- Selfishness—always putting yourself first

neck your ego at the door and consider putting others before urself. This is a lesson I've learned many times in business. It's a ecurring lesson, as a matter of fact, the "gift" that keeps on giving!

During my time at one of the top management consulting firms in the world, I worked with an exceptionally bright consultant. My colleague was book-smart, emotionally intelligent and confident. She was so confident, she was completely unafraid to admit when she didn't know something. In those cases, here's what she would say to a client: "I don't know the answer to that question right now but give me a few hours. I will research, analyze, and find supporting resources to give you the facts by the end of the day."

Boom! What a great way to approach things. This shows humility, intelligence, and a person who is in charge. These words are devoid of ego or boastfulness, and they're meant to put the needs of the client first. An imperative in business! If we always lead with our needs and don't think of anyone but ourselves, we'll miss out on some wonderful friendships and relationships. We grow through mutually beneficial social interaction. We learn so much more about ourselves by listening with genuine interest to friends and business colleagues. We begin to find out more answers to questions that have eluded us.

We're never going to have all the answers in this lifetime—it's a fool's errand to pretend that we will. There's a lot we don't know. But it's better to build relationships and learn from others. We do that by putting those people first. When we keep our eyes and ears open and live with humility, we become more of the person we desire to be.

Value within the Value

" *You find that being vulnerable is the only way to allow your heart to feel true pleasure that's so real, it scares you."—Bob Marley*

Personal growth comes when you operate without regard for what you will receive. That tends to take care of itself when you lead with noble intentions, authenticity, and a smile on your face. Selfish motivation and thinking only about yourself are a prescription for failure. But that's not always the way it's portrayed in the media or the content we consume.

We live in a 24/7 world of social media and tabloid-headlines. When we see people garnering attention for doing things that are totally self-centered, it feels unfair. A "me-first" culture exists, which enforces and rewards selfish behavior. This engenders a sense of pleasure and self-gratification that is hard to resist. We all fall victim to it at one point or another. Unfortunately, we sometimes think first of ourselves and second ... of ourselves. And third ... well you get the picture. The people closest to us then take a backseat to any ambition and venture we pursue for ourselves.

So, how do we turn this around? Living with humility isn't easy. In fact, of all the values, humility is often the hardest to embrace. Being humble requires that we overcome ourselves, to become ourselves. What do I mean? To be humble, we must be vulnerable. When we're vulnerable, we take a courageous step forward in showing our emotions. We bare our souls, show our faults and in turn, make others comfortable to show theirs. We let others see our authenticity. Traits like vulnerability and humility were once scorned and viewed as signs of weakness. Not anymore. Humility is

...n of courage. While we have a long way to go as a society, there . plenty of people like you and me who embrace a humble mindset nd share it with their co-workers and friends.

I think back to the woman who hired me for my first job in business. A senior leader, she was an unassuming, quiet woman. You would have thought she was one of your subordinates, rather than your manager. She was very graceful and caring of others. She never spoke about herself. Instead, she wanted to hear how everyone else was doing. She put herself out there, vulnerable and humble, and never expected much in return. Her example left an indelible impact on the way I treat others.

> " *The highest type of ruler is one of whose existence the people are barely aware.*"—Lao-Tzu, Tao te Ching

She went out of her way to meet everyone she managed and took employees out to lunch early on during their tenure with the company. She surrounded herself with a loving family at home. That beautiful love in her personal life carried over, flowing into her professional life. She kept things positive, and treated others with humility that let everyone know she cared.

Get to know the people you lead and surround yourself with. Don't just engage in small talk that borders on the trivial. Think of how many conversations you have about the weather. You might feel like you have a Ph.D. in meteorology by now! Leave that to Al Roker, instead. Meaningful relationships are what matter most. Show people that you care about them. Show you're willing to put them first. That is the mark of a true leader. Great leaders are humble, vulnerable, and unselfish. Ultimately, they thrive by exhibiting this beh[...] and they earn the respect of all.

The Experts

There are people on TV spouting off about which way the stock market will go and how the weather will be tomorrow. These people get paid lots of money to be ... wrong. Over. And. Over. Again. Weather forecasters are wrong seemingly more often than they're right. That rainstorm you didn't expect to ruin your child's birthday party on Friday? Oops, it came a bit early. Sorry 'bout that. And as for the stock market, I'll leave it to Peter Lynch—a famous investor considered a financial markets legend of his own time—to speak to that: "Nobody can predict interest rates, the future direction of the economy, or the stock market."[3]

Well, then. There go our retirement accounts!

There's so much that so many people are wrong about, yet they're far too proud to admit it. They're not necessarily wrong because someone else is right, but because they simply don't know. Our society has become a culture of "experts." Professing to know it all can get us far, but only when we actually know the answers—not when we're just guessing.

But I don't really care about a stock picker or a weather forecaster. I'm concerned with you and me. Some of us walk around 24/7 acting like we know it all, without ever challenging ourselves to think deeper about the facts—to seek the truth. I acknowledge there are things that I don't have a clue about. But I didn't always feel this way. For a long time in my twenties, I was the angry young man that Billy Joel once crooned about. I thought I knew everything. I took my e from a prestigious liberal arts college and walked around with smug opinions, airing them to any fool who would listen.

I'm eternally grateful no one recorded me during one of my philosophical rants on how much I *thought* I knew. At least I hope no one did. (If you have the tapes, please, surrender them immediately!) What I didn't know then is that there is tremendous power in admitting we're wrong—having the self-awareness to recognize that we don't know it all. Sound familiar?

Many of us were taught growing up to put on a brave face and "tough things out." Some of us were raised to think if we asked a basic question or two, it would make us look bad. Once we reach adulthood, we assume when we don't know something, it's a sign of weakness to our bosses, girlfriends, professors, peers, or classmates. Far from it.

Intellectual curiosity shows a hungry, humble person searching for answers. Sign those people up on my team any day of the week. We need to scratch the itch so we can find out the truth—the real answers to what we don't know. The tipping point of this personal discovery is simple: humility in thought and action. Maturity means that on occasion, we eat some good old-fashioned humble pie. And that's okay. Build humility into your values structure and begin anew the quest for VERITAS—the truth.

Results of Humility

> **"***I have three precious things which I hold fast and prize. The first is gentleness; the second is frugality; the third is humility, which keeps me from putting myself before others. Be gentle and you can*

be bold; be frugal and you can be liberal; avoid putting yourse~~r~~
fore others and you can become a leader..." — Lao Tzu

The results of humility, when properly managed in you.
emotional, mental, and spiritual approach to living, are shared
respect by your peers and an openness to doing the right thing. Like
all values, humility is an inward transformation that is observed
externally by friends, family, co-workers, and perfect strangers.

When I coach clients and teams, I often tell people to be humbly
confident. It's not an oxymoron. Humble confidence is recognizing
our faults and areas for improvement, while still leading with our
strengths. It's a mindset of powerful belief in self that inspires the
way we treat others. False humility or overly humble behavior is
detracting and leads to a lack of self-confidence. It shows a lack of
self-awareness. As a result, it leaves us susceptible to being taken
advantage of by others who don't fully realize the intentions of our
hearts. So much of the enjoyment, success, and fulfillment of life
comes through building authentic relationships both in our personal
and professional lives.

We do so with kindness, humility and confidence. When we lack
even one of these values, we run the risk of losing our potential
audience. This may be a future girlfriend, who could become our
wife. This may be an opportunity for a young artist looking to sell
her idea to a person of influence that falls through, because of poor
body language or manners.

Be humble, gracious, and kind, but never mistake this for the need
to be overly humble. Generally speaking, too much of anything is not
a good thing! The result of humility, when balanced with other

s, is the recognition of your authenticity and genuineness, ding to the exact type of representation you want others to see in ou.

Opportunity is more likely to come your way when you're prepared. The best way to prepare is by fusing your heart's desire with your mind's thoughts to adopt a humble approach of servant leadership toward others. Take care of yourself and keep growing, but build into your routine the desire and willingness to act for the greater good of others. It is undeniably the case that opportunity will come knocking once you've humbly served others before yourself.

Game Plan

1. Think about the activities that leave you feeling self-absorbed. This could be spending too much time on your smartphone, or binge-watching that "must-see" series on Netflix. Consider investing that time in others. Use the time you would otherwise use on yourself to humbly serve someone else.

2. Be willing to admit when you're wrong. If you don't have the answer, don't be afraid to say, "I don't know." Humility drives personal development because it leads to a hunger for knowledge. If you want to learn and grow, you need to strengthen your strengths and improve your weaknesses. Know what those are.

Notes

[1] "Humility," Merriam-Webster, https://www.merriam-webster.com/dictionary/humility (accessed May 27, 2017).

[2] "Humble," *Merriam-Webster*, https://www.merriam-webster.com/dictionary/humble (accessed May 27, 2017).

[3] Peter Lynch, *Beating the Street* (New York: Simon & Schuster, 1993), 317 (paperback edition).

CHAPTER 21

Fun

"Fun is one of the most important—and underrated—ingredients in any successful venture. If you're not having fun, then it's probably time to call it quits and try something else."

— *Richard Branson*

<u>**DEFINITION:**</u>

(1) What provides amusement or enjoyment: playful often boisterous action or speech[1]

(2) A mood for finding or making amusement

Get in a relaxed, happy state of mind. No worries, palm trees, soft sand, a calm breeze as the waves gently push upon the shore. No, this isn't an infomercial for a Caribbean vacation. Just trying to get you in a good mood! Think about the moment in your day or time of the week that you know will bring you enjoyment. These are the times we build toward and look forward to most. Let me take it a step further—what was the most fun day of your life? Think about it. Here's mine:

The most fun day of my life was October 20, 2012. It was the day I took my wife's hand in marriage, and then celebrated with 100 of closest family and friends. From the church to the reception, the was designed as a celebration of love and fun. It was awesome to celebrate and share that day with the closest people in our lives. Maybe you know the feeling. I wanted to immerse myself completely in that experience. The fun, laughs, and good times rolled. I never wanted it to end, knowing, of course, that all good things do come to an end.

Life's greatest gifts are the times shared with the people we love most. This is when we laugh, celebrate, and thoroughly enjoy each other's company. Being part of a beautiful wedding with heartfelt vows, music, and an indescribable feeling of love in the air is a memory I treasure. Your definition of fun may be going to a Kenny Chesney concert, tailgating at your favorite football team's big game, or lighting up the dancefloor at one of your favorite clubs. It doesn't have to be an event. It could just be a home-cooked meal with family, loving one another's company with joy in your heart.

Fun helps give meaning to our lives, allowing us that time for happiness, laughs, and the experience of truly living in the moment. Think about those times. Whether it's your wedding or getting an ice cream cone with your sister or son, find your fun.

The Core of Fun

If we're all business and no play, where's the fun in that? Fun adds humor and joy to our lives. We all realize this, yet too often we build a life where fun tends to be at opposite ends of the spectrum: either it gets squeezed out of our schedule entirely, or we turn away from our obligations and have too much fun. Fun should be the time each week where we kick back, unwind, and chill to help relieve some

stress and share a laugh with friends or loved ones. This is our b.
from all the distractions and mundane parts of our daily and weer
life.

Fun is about immersion in a given moment, letting loose and
having a good time. You may have your fun sharing a great laugh with
old friends at a get-together or watching your son or daughter jump
for joy in the bouncy house at an indoor amusement park. Part of
having fun is expressing your willingness to be yourself. When
you're not being yourself, life is so much harder. When you try on
someone else's skin thinking it will fit, all it ends up doing is covering
over the real you. The times we try living someone else's life,
thinking it will be fun, we usually end up unhappy. Our destiny is
fulfilled when we figure out how to blend enthusiasm and fun into
our lives each day.

66 *Be yourself; everyone else is already taken."* [2] *—Oscar Wilde*

Fun and humor break up the serious moments and provide us
with clarity of thought that enlightens our mood and perspective. It's
no secret that some of the most memorable moments of our lives are
the times when we had the most fun. Maybe we reminisced with
loved ones or we visited a brilliant, new place for the first time and
let the magic of that setting wash over us in vibrant emotion.

As you focus on the importance of values and personal
development, view fun as the buddy that accompanies you on your
journey. No matter how serious life gets, it's always important to
smile and have fun. When we were younger, our parents initiated
play time that brought us together with friends for hours at a time.
Little did we know, but these were huge moments of development

our brains. There's every reason to believe these same moments continue to keep our brains actively functioning as we get older.

According to Dr. Sergio Pellis, a researcher at the University of Lethbridge in Alberta, Canada: "The experience of play changes the connections of the neurons at the front end of your brain. And without play experience, those neurons aren't changed."[3]

In an article citing Dr. Pellis, NPR writer Jon Hamilton adds: "It is those changes in the prefrontal cortex during childhood that help wire up the brain's executive control center, which has a critical role in regulating emotions, making plans and solving problems, Pellis says. So play, he adds, is what prepares a young brain for life, love and even schoolwork."[4]

Stay active and find the time for amusement, laughs, and joy. It will add value and rhythm to your life. Play time isn't just for kids, it's also for adults. We have to laugh and have a good time. Even if it's at our own expense!

Obstacles to Living with Fun

❝ *Humor is perhaps a sense of intellectual perspective: an awareness that some things are really important, others not; and that the two kinds are most oddly jumbled in everyday affairs."— Christopher Morley*

- Taking each moment or ourselves too seriously

- Lack of planning and imagination

- Fear of letting loose

- Difficult circumstances

- Expecting to always have fun

We can't always expect fun around every corner. Life is not one, constant series of fun meant only to entertain and bring us joy twenty-four hours per day. To anyone who's ever experienced low points or disappointments, no matter how big or small, we know occasional downs are part of the course of life. We should treasure the awesome, inspiring moments of fun and happiness and let them sprinkle our lives with hope. This way, we set a baseline to cherish these moments, so we can look back upon them with a smile and joyful heart.

Great times are also a reminder that there is a tremendous amount in life to be happy and grateful for, if we take time to meditate on those moments and plan them out. Let's focus on the wonderful, happy occasions that bring a smile to our faces and joy to our hearts. Commit these times to memory because there will be times of suffering and sorrow in life. These times, like a death in the family or recovery from an injury, help us see how much we should cherish moments of joy.

Fun and happiness are the threads we want intertwined throughout our life experiences to the greatest degree possible. Don't worry about letting loose and busting a funky move out on that dancefloor, player! Poke fun at yourself every now and then. There are times to be serious and times to tell a self-deprecating joke that loosens up a whole room of strangers. I happen to be a big practitioner of the latter! Don't let the obstacles hold you back. Be

...dful of fun and how it will make your life and the ones around ...u better.

Value within the Value

66 *Never, ever underestimate the importance of having fun.*"— *Randy Pausch*

At the beginning of each year, like many people, I write out a list of New Year's Resolutions. I'm not only looking to patch up the holes—to remedy my weaknesses—I'm trying to strengthen my strengths and improve what I'm best at. I'm looking for an edge—more ways that I can add value to all that I do. This is serious work! Yet, I make a point of writing these words on every edition of my annual resolutions:

Don't forget to HAVE FUN!

I want to work hard and accomplish my goals, but I absolutely want to have fun doing it. Without fun, everything would feel like an obligation. Life's more rewarding when achieving goals feels like something to look forward to, rather than a chore to avoid.

As you examine your life, focus on what needs to be done, but make sure to have a healthy dose of fun while you're at it. Make sure the activities that give meaning to your life lead to fun and enthusiasm. Celebrate the "fun time," don't take it for granted. Enjoy the light-hearted moments of life. At least once per week, turn on the TV to a comedy or program that is sure to make you laugh. Watch old video clips on the Internet that make you smile. Make it a par~~t~~ your routine to ensure you don't take yourself too seriously!

A Story to Tell

Midway through my sophomore year of college, I gave up playing basketball for my school team. This was one of the toughest decisions of my life. I had played from the time I could barely walk. Other than my faith and relationship with my family, basketball was the biggest part of my life. Playing the game, going to camps, working on my own to improve my skills and abilities, this was what dominated my youth. And very suddenly, it was gone. I took myself out. I simply wasn't having fun anymore.

I was recruited to play basketball by several colleges. My dream was always to play college basketball, and I was driven and motivated to achieve it. Basketball was fun. It was my competitive outlet, the activity that revved up my engine and ignited the fire within me. I loved the camaraderie of the game and being a part of a team. But playing college basketball was anything but a good time. It felt like an unpaid internship with mean co-workers. Basketball had always been fun. Then, suddenly, it no longer was. I gave my all during drills, practices, and game preparation, but when my freshman season ended, I took a long break.

I came back to campus in the fall excited for school to begin, but not as much for basketball season. As tryouts started, the expectation was that I would become a reliable rotation player. Little did they know; my career was coming to an end. Tryouts were usually a mere formality for scholarship players. I vividly remember during tryouts feeling like I wanted to be elsewhere. One of our assistant coaches

..iced and asked me: "Chris, do you want to be here?" I didn't ..nswer. My silence spoke volumes. A few days later, I was cut. And while the competitor in me was disappointed, the part of me that simply wanted to enjoy college was relieved.

I entered a very confounding time on my college journey. But as the saying goes, when one door closes, another one opens. And that it did. One month earlier, I started my college broadcasting career, following in my brother's footsteps by announcing college sports on the radio. Later, I became the sports director of my college radio station. It was the most rewarding, and fun experience of my college years. I gained valuable experience broadcasting major college sports events, traveling, and managing staff. It's still one of my favorite life experiences.

When you're moving fast, never slowing down, do yourself a favor and stop for a minute to recharge your battery. You might find you're not enjoying life the way you should. Take a deep breath and remember me telling you: **Don't forget to have fun!**

Results of Fun

> *Laugh as much as possible, always laugh. It's the sweetest thing one can do for oneself and one's fellow human beings."— Maya Angelou*

My wife and I love to do ridiculous impressions. Given my New York upbringing and her southern roots, we tend to take on opposite roles. It's worked well, since she lived on my turf in New York for three years, while we now make our home in South Carolina. It gets particularly silly when she starts impersonating famous people with New York accents, like Bernie Sanders or Sylvester Stallone. Take my word for it, listening to a southern belle try and put on her best older man's New York accent is well worth your time—and perhaps even a price for admission!

Part of our special bond—our camaraderie—together as a married couple is the ability to make each other laugh. There's nothing that gives my wife a laugh quite like when I break into my impersonation of a southern debutante. And likewise, my wife usually leaves me gasping for a breath when she tries her Rocky Balboa impression, talking tough to Ivan Drago or Clubber Lang. Those moments, when we stare into each other's eyes and laugh so hard we beg for oxygen, are among my favorite in all of life. They're special to us. They're unique and they bring joy to our hearts. I bet you have these moments with your friends, partners, and loved ones. Keep 'em going.

Ask yourself if you have time each week for fun. If not, then what's the point? In the end, your most competitive endeavors, pursuits of passion, or time with family should all be in the spirit of fun. It's valuable to extract meaning and wisdom from your experiences, as I advocate throughout this book. But there's also a time to mix in some fun and keep things loose. The journey of personal discovery and the development of core values is not a witch hunt or a blame-game for all that we've done wrong. We can't try to lift ourselves up while simultaneously tearing ourselves down! We're moving toward positivity and pluses, so we must not let the negatives subtract from our progress.

Don't pick apart mistakes or foolish things you did. Laugh at them and realize life isn't always a "repair job" of everything you did wrong. Life is meant to be fun. I encourage you: find your fun

.10ments, among family, friends, your partner, or even strangers. Inject some humor and a light-hearted joke here and there at your job to keep everyone smiling. I vividly recall some of the jokes and fun ribbing I heard during my days working on the floor of the New York Stock Exchange. It was a fast-paced, highly competitive environment with lots of egos—and even more money at stake. But you would have thought it was a comedy club at times. The best medicine for shaking things up was often a well-timed joke.

It's those times that we'll never forget. They add splashes of color to a life that on occasion can have its black and white moments. Watch a good comedy now and then. Crack a joke. Have the humility to laugh at yourself. Enjoy life. It's more fun that way.

Game Plan

1. Take a big-picture view at your week. What are you doing for fun or what have you planned for fun in the long term? I use a calendar that allows me to group my tasks by categories. I have a category specifically labeled "Fun." And oh yeah, its color is yellow. This is where I plan times to go to sporting events, dinner, concerts, vacations, and simple things that I know will bring happiness and enjoyment to my family. Life goes by so fast, and sometimes we literally forget to plan time in for fun. When you plan it, you think about it, and then you act upon it.

2. Decide when to have fun and when to focus on your job and personal goals. It's a difficult balance but it's absolutely possible to have both. When you're ahead of the game, you can mix business with pleasure. You don't always have to

drop one to have the other. Work toward what you want to be and focus on your goals. But take a break here and there to have fun. Celebrate the big victories and small wins in life.

Notes

[1] "Fun," *Merriam-Webster*, https://www.merriam-webster.com/dictionary/fun (accessed May 21, 2017).

[2] Quote generally attributed to Oscar Wilde, source unknown.

[3] Sergio Pellis, quoted in Jon Hamilton, "Scientists Say Child's Play Helps Build A Better Brain," NPR, August 6, 2014, http://www.npr.org/sections/ed/2014/08/06/336361277/scientists-say-childs-play-helps-build-a-better-brain (accessed May 21, 2017).

[4] Ibid.

The Journey Forward

I started this book by taking you on a journey. I close, not with an end, but rather with your beginning. This is your time. You made a commitment when you opened this book and turned to the first page to begin reading. Keep the momentum going. Take this feeling of empowerment and surge forward. Start your journey.

Living by values is an everyday commitment. There are times it will be easy and at times it will be hard. It's easy to live by values when it's convenient. We all want to stand in the winner's circle and celebrate the victories and good times of life. That's easy! Just know that life will always throw challenges your way. How you respond is everything. The more you run away from life's challenges, the tougher it gets. As you've learned, facing and overcoming adversity becomes easy once you realize adversity is your best friend.

Here are your two biggest challenges:

1. Getting started (Beginning)
2. Living every day by values (Repetition)

We all have to begin somewhere. It's nearly impossible to begin when we have no guiding purpose—no reason for doing. Many of us start down paths without a plan or goal in mind, and we don't do the all-important work of questioning ourselves or contemplating why we're unhappy. It isn't until days, months or even years pass that we realize the direction we're headed isn't good enough. Yet there's always an opportunity to stop. We can always change our course. As the great Robert Plant famously said, "Yes, there are two paths you can go by, but in the long run there's still time to change the road you're on."

The incredible part of life is that you can always start over. Starting over isn't about beginning a new job or finding a new partner. Starting over begins in your mind, once you're willing to accept the challenge of becoming everything you've always wanted to be.

Home Base

Come back to this book when you've strayed. Come back to it for guidance and reassurance, even when you know you're on the right path. Come back to it for a refresher before that big job interview, or a dose of confidence before the final exam. When the rhythm of your daily life doesn't quite feel complete, maybe you simply need to rely more on a value like optimism or fire—ones that may have eluded you.

Values are not a one-time deal. They're not a box you check, move on from and never come back to. When leveraged properly, values last a lifetime. They become ingrained in our minds and actions. We realize the way we think and what we do are a byproduct of the values we hold dear. Living a life of values takes time. It takes refinement in approach, which comes with practice—and practice makes perfect.

Think about it—when you've lived by time-tested values like the ones in this book, how have things worked out for you? I'm guessing, quite well. I know it's worked out well for me. Let me just get one thing straight: living a life of values does not mean living a perfect life. As you've seen from my story, as well as the myriad other stories in this book, there's no such thing as a perfect life. Life is chock full of mistakes. And ironically, maybe the closest thing to a perfect life is one where we make many mistakes. Because it is through mistakes that we learn and become the best version of ourselves.

Looking Back to Look Forward

Living a life with values is for everyone. It's all-inclusive. Values don't discriminate based on age, race, gender or religion. Values simply require you to stay true to yourself. You'll be tempted to try on someone else's life and make the mistake of thinking it's yours. Emulate, admire and then move forward with what you've learned. Observe and borrow from others, but stay laser-focused on bringing it back to your course. The self-improvement steps laid out in this book will take time to be realized. Your growth will happen on your time because your life and experiences are truly unique.

Look back at your past experiences. Think of what you've learned, when you've succeeded and when you've failed. What lessons can you take from each of those experiences? What about the people who have meant the most to you? What have they left you with? What experiences have resonated with you?

We learned through the pages of this book that Michael Jordan got knocked down throughout his career, before he reached the summit of stardom. He got there by outworking the competition and living each day with a burning fire to be the best. We found through J. K. Rowling's story that hope is an eternal flame which lights the way toward victory. We learned that love is a value inside all of us. We can commit to loving our neighbor every day with an open heart. And we found through courage and altruism that sometimes, the greatest love of all is risking everything—even our lives—for the good of others.

Living a life of values, on your terms, requires that you take chances. You must be willing to give things a shot! You'll find that playing things conservatively isn't bad from time to time, but it's also not a winning long-term strategy. Like with anything, there has to be balance. You have to be willing to push yourself into new ways of thinking and living. Perseverance pushes you beyond the limits of where you previously may have quit. Open-mindedness allows you to entertain possibilities and opportunities. A willingness to compete will keep you on the playing field and off the sidelines. The range of values put forth in this book will help to define your purpose and increase your appetite for taking worthy chances.

Let this book be the foundation on which you build your new life. You'll need a powerful structure to navigate the changes of life. President John F. Kennedy once said, "Change is the law of life. And those who look only to the past or present are certain to miss the future." You need something to keep you grounded, to keep guiding you and moving you toward your goals, when life continues to change all around you. Values are there as you mature and discover yourself. Values are your compass when the external world seems bent on pushing you off-course. Values will be there through it all.

As you look back at where you've been and where you are now, I ask that you look forward with joy and love in your hearts and confidence and faith in your thoughts. Values will take you to where you've always believed you can go. But you'll need more than that. You'll need a plan to get there. And you must not hesitate or delay— you must be willing to act! The path to mediocrity is trodden by those who never had a plan. My big hopes and dreams started to come true because I built my plan and foundation on values. I hope you'll start your plan the same way.

Begin your journey. You get to decide what it will look like. From there, you can get started on writing—or re-writing—your future. Only you can be the author. It's your turn. It's your time. Write your masterpiece.

Acknowledgements

From the bottom of my heart, I thank God for leading me to publish this book. The man I am today is because of His grace, love and guidance. This book is a tribute to God and hopefully, a small token of gratitude to show appreciation for my reliance on God's strength and wisdom.

To my wife, you are my rock and I thank you for your love, friendship and for standing by me through everything. You believed in me, when I didn't believe in myself. Thank you for always being my love and for supporting my dreams. I'm so excited for our future. To my son Roman, I love you more than you will ever know. You inspired me to write this book. You bring so much joy, love and optimism to my life! To quote John Lennon, "I can hardly wait, to see you come of age." My beautiful boy.

I'm grateful to my parents for all their love, friendship, mentoring and faith in me. What can I say? I hit the lottery when God awarded me with you two as parents. I'll never be able to repay you for all you've done for me. I just hope I can make you proud and be half the parent to my children that you two have been for me. I love you and thank you for everything you've done—and continue to do—for me.

To my brother Kevin—you've always been a huge inspiration and model for me. I greatly admire your professionalism, faith and perseverance. Thank you for being such an amazing mentor, brother and dear friend. I love you. To my brother, Bill- thank you for your marketing expertise and willingness to help. You're a great friend. Your belief and confidence in me means more than you'll ever know. I'm truly grateful for your generosity and for always having my back.

To my editors, Darcie Clemen and Mary Beth Baker: Your professional and personal guidance helped make this book the product I'm so proud of. Thank you for your time, effort and help in making me a better writer! To Brian Punger, my cover and interior designer, you are a pro and a good friend. Thank you for your countless hours spent on turning this book into a great product. I appreciate all your hard work and diligence in making this dream become a reality.

To my late grandmother, Mary, who helped instill faith in me and taught me so much about living by values. You are missed every day, but never forgotten. To my Uncle Owen—thank you for being such a great friend and loving Uncle. You are missed.

To my godparents, Brian and Kathy. Thank you always for your love and support of my dreams!

Thank you to everyone who reviewed this book and took the time to offer honest feedback. It has made all the difference. To all of my extended family and friends, past and present, and to all my co-workers and colleagues, thanks for your guidance. To everyone who ever helped me on my way, I'm grateful to you. I'll never forget it. Know that you always have a friend who will have your back and help you when you ask.

To all my followers and fans near and far, thank you. I'll always stay true to myself and give you the best I have. I get to live out my dream. I'm a lucky man. Thanks for letting me spread my message of values, positivity and empowerment across the globe!

Continue Your Journey

Blog: Come visit Christopher's website at http://chrisdconnors.com and subscribe to the *Live Boldly* newsletter. Christopher's writing is featured on his website and at medium.com/@chrisdconnors.

LinkedIn: linkedin.com/in/chrisdconnors

Twitter: twitter.com/Chris_Connors42

Facebook: facebook.com/chrisdconnors

Instagram: instagram.com/chrisdconnors

Speaking: Book Christopher for your next conference or event! Contact him via his website and provide speaking details and contact information: http://chrisdconnors.com

Just looking to say, Hi? Reach out and contact Christopher via his website anytime: www.chrisdconnors.com

Personal Game Plan

So, how do you begin your personal game plan? With a foundation of core values, of course! But how do you build from there? Here is the start of your plan. This is how to begin crafting the written promise to hold yourself accountable.

1. **Your Definition of Success** (What success means for you)

2. **Success Measures** (The ways to determine whether you're living up to your definition of success)

3. **Your Why** (Why you're doing, what you're doing)

4. **Goals** (The results you hope to achieve through your efforts)

5. **Strengths and Areas for Improvement** (Honestly assess your strengths and determine the areas where there is room for growth)

6. **List of Excuses** (We all have excuses; list yours. Then, one-by-one, determine how you will overcome and eliminate what is holding you back)

Believe

My Mom gave me this poem several years ago during a very challenging time of adversity in my life. I've kept it in my wallet and I turn to it for inspiration and hope. It has meant everything to me. I hope this helps to give life to the value of faith and all other values for you.

Believe in yourself –
in the power you have
to control your own life, day by day,
Believe in the strength
that you have deep inside,
and your faith will help
show you the way.
Believe in tomorrow
and what it will bring -
let a hopeful heart carry you through,
For things will work out
if you trust and believe
there's no limit
to what you can do.

\-   *Emily Matthews*

About the Author

Christopher D. Connors is an author, writer, coach and business consultant who has worked with senior executives in the federal government and at Fortune 500 companies. His writing has appeared in *CNBC*, *HuffPost*, *Thought Catalog* and *Medium*. He has appeared as a guest on *Sirius XM* radio. Christopher is a highly sought-after speaker among millennials and professionals in the business, academic and nonprofit world. His core message of building a personal game plan on core values resonates with thousands. Christopher is happily married to his awesome wife and is the proud father of a rambunctious, baseball-loving toddler. He lives in Charleston, South Carolina. Visit him at chrisdconnors.com